The Nameless Social Worker

The Nameless Social Worker

RACHEL BRAMBLE

JANUS PUBLISHING COMPANY
London, England

First Published in Great Britain 2004
by Janus Publishing Company Ltd,
105-107 Gloucester Place,
London W1U 6BY

www.januspublishing.co.uk

British Library Cataloguing-in-Publication Data
A catalogue record for this book
is available from the British Library

ISBN 1 85756 519 3

Cover Design Simon Hughes

Printed and bound in Great Britain

Prologue

I live in a village just a few miles from Stafford with my two children. This is the story of my life so far, that is until the age of forty-seven years. I am just an ordinary woman but I think that the people who have shaped my life deserve their fifteen minutes of fame.

I am the nameless social worker but only one of many. Each of us has interesting tales to tell and so I would like to dedicate this book to everyone who has shaped my life.

I am writing this book not out of a sense of vanity but because I fear for the future of many people in society. There are many people who need the support of social workers but are fearful of approaching Social Services because of the poor public image and the stigma that they feel they will carry around with them.

One day I took a client whose child is on the child protection register to see a friend of hers. The friend had a big smile and a hug waiting for her but she immediately told me that she had been "under" Social Services as a child and that she had been separated from her siblings and had not seen one of them for years. I listened to this tale and sympathised with her. She thought that this time felt as if it were a prison sentence and that now she was released. I couldn't blame her though, as sometimes that is the way I see it too. Not because of goodwill but because of the bureaucracy that surrounds all the work.

A few days later we had a discussion in the office about a psychiatrist who had suggested to a family with an autistic child that, because they were embarrassed by his behaviour in public, he should wear a T-shirt which said "I am autistic and proud of it". I, like the other social workers, was appalled by the idea and had visions of all individuals who were a bit of a "nuisance" through circumstances beyond their control wearing such T-shirts. If this was the scenario, all the people with dementia would wear a T-shirt saying "Please excuse me because I am demented".

I felt that it was because the public didn't know enough about autism that it was a problem. The idea just sent shivers down my spine and stirred thoughts of Big Brother.

However, the truth is that social workers are fearful of the media and deliberately avoid any contact with newspapers, TV and radio unless it is for a specific reason, such as recruiting foster parents. Consequently, the media have no interest in us and the people we work with. If TV programmes fully represented the general population, then on a regular basis we would see more children with autism or elderly people with dementia. Social workers become the nameless people who strive each day to improve the lives of the people we work with and to keep them safe. We do this with the kind of resources that large companies would laugh at, and the extent of bureaucracy which entangles us in a thick web created by an unknowing hierarchy. Our government and our people really know very little of what we do.

Of six hundred and fifty-nine MPs that I wrote to in February 2002 about our relationship with the media (see letter to MPs in Part II), five hundred have still not bothered to even acknowledge my letter. So how can they condemn what we do, and what right do they have to create an even larger web of bureaucracy? How much do they even care?

This book is about my life and the many people I have worked with. They deserve to have their stories told. It is a combination of thoughts and actions and is interspersed with happenings, and as such shows the ever-changing nature of the life of a social worker.

Part I is the story of my life to the age of forty-seven and the people that have shaped who I am. It is also about emotions and is interspersed with real-life happenings and feelings, as well as strong powerful memories.

Part II is about ideas and thoughts concerning social work – my thoughts, which have never been tested or previously published, and how and why they came about.

This book is alive and evolving, and so at times feels disjointed. I am trying to give a sense of time and so will try not to edit it too heavily. I hope that it will get published – I hope by an expert who will give me advice on how to distribute it effectively. I want to give people the opportunity to challenge my thoughts and ideas but also to give other social workers the confidence to have a go, to tell the world what is really happening in the social work profession.

The Nameless Social Worker is dedicated to my late husband, Tim, who was a part of my life for so long and who sadly died in March 2001. He introduced me to the character of Dilbert, who, through his author, said what he thought without worrying what other people thought. Tim was a clever computer worker who could solve many a hitch in the computer world. Unfortunately, the pressures of life meant that after twenty-four years I had to leave him to make a better life for myself and my children, but we were still in close contact right to the end. I only wish that I had persuaded him to leave the rat race. Life is full of regrets but I will try my best to open the eyes of the public to the truth about social work. And I thank Tim for his love and for the finances to get this book published.

Part I – The Beginning

Introduction

Phoebe knocks the door at 6.45am, walks in with a tray, which turns out to be an oven tray, and sings "Happy Birthday" to me.

On the oven tray is a bowl with tinned pears and Ideal milk, a Langley Farm raspberry yogurt, a carton of orange, lemon and pineapple drink, and a Cadbury's Snowflake. With it she has a home-made birthday card with a pop-up heart in the middle and two little plastic bags. One contains two hair clips and two red hearts. The other contains one pink, one yellow and one blue bath bomb.

She says the bath bombs are because I enjoy having baths, the clips are because I like messing with my hair and the hearts are because I apparently always say that I want love on my birthday and that it is the best present in the world.

I ate my delicious breakfast before Phoebe had to go to catch her 7.30am bus to school.

Just after Phoebe leaves for school I hear a lot of commotion upstairs from Joshua's bedroom and a few minutes later he walks in carrying his army rucksack. He says "happy birthday" and passes it to me and tells me to look inside. Inside there are three blue and three green bottles of bubble bath. There is also a huge bar of chocolate.

This is so much about my children, so different, so special.

In all the excitement I forget to take Stephen the ritual morning cup of coffee. I go upstairs and hidden away he has an enormous bouquet of flowers with lovely smiling sunflowers amongst them, a bottle of champagne and *The Story of Flight 93*. What a fantastic start to my birthday.

Yesterday I carried out a supervision contact between a woman who has been labelled as difficult, and her mildly disabled son. She shares my birthday and I wonder how her day is starting. I am also working with a woman who has four children, only one of whom lives with her. One of her children shares Phoebe's birthday, which is tomorrow.

As I looked back on my forty-seven years I reflect on the good and the bad times, but more importantly I think about why I had to write this book. Why I had to share my life with the world and why *The Nameless Social Worker* had to be its title.

My name is Rachel but not Bramble – that is fiction, but everything else that I have written about is fact. Names may have been changed along the way to protect people.

My life is my life and is not typical or atypical of a social worker, but what writing this has shown is the desperate need for the public to wake up. We can no longer live in a fantasy world where everything is fantastic and someone else deals with the sorrow and hardship. We all have to do our share because otherwise we will lose our humanness.

Chapter 1 – Not a Care in the World

One of the Baby Boomers

I was born on 27th September 1955 to Lizzie and Matthew. I have two older brothers, Luke and Edmund. Both Edmund and I were born in Birmingham, but Luke was born in Romford.

Mum and Dad met just after the war. Mum still has the first letter that Dad sent to her, which is lovely. It talks about how he liked the look of her, and said that if she liked the look of him could he meet her in the centre of Bristol.

They had their fiftieth wedding anniversary three years ago. At the beginning of writing this book my father died from prostate cancer.

I was born into an upper-middle-class family. My paternal grandfather was a Professor of Botany at Bristol University and has been one of the most influential people in my life. He died when I was seventeen years old.

He taught me how exciting the world is and how you can be interested in all sorts of things. At times I wished that I had his brain. He was a very clever man. He published books when he was in his twenties, he was a scientist, was good at languages, and was really very clever at all sorts of things – except crossing roads. He came to live in Birmingham when I was eight years old and I spent a lot of time with him. One day he got knocked down in the centre of Birmingham, but fortunately he was okay. After that, if we were out walking together and he was near the road I would tell him to stay on the path. He was also rather eccentric; he made his own jam and, much to my embarrassment, would often pick fruit from trees along the street where we lived.

When I was about thirteen years old I asked him what syphilis was. He explained in a totally unembarrassed way. This, at times, makes me cringe now, as in those days and even now it would not be regarded as decent conversation between a thirteen-year-old and her granddad who was in his seventies. Not only did he tell me what it was but a few days later I was given an academic lecture about its origins – I was fascinated.

Granddad taught me something, which I have retained in life: if you take an interest in what people are good at then you will find the best in them.

I am not saying that everything was rosy between me and Granddad, because as I got older sometimes I would be embarrassed by him just like any other kid and their elders, but on the whole this was not the case.

He also did get rather forgetful. For example, he liked to give me seasonal treats but when I received a pomegranate every day for two weeks I had to go to Mum for help. I think that it is really hard to eat a whole pomegranate every day with a cocktail stick, which is what we did in those days.

You may wonder where my mum and dad fit into the story. Well I have been extremely lucky on the whole to have parents who love me and have always been there for me. They have been very tolerant and were progressive for their time.

Dad worked at Birmingham University and some Saturdays me, Mum and my brothers would go to meet him and have our dinner in Staff House.

If he was finishing off his work, sometimes Luke, Edmund and I would go in different people's offices and telephone each other. We found this really exciting. We got to meet all sorts of people at the university and were really not in awe of any academics. At periodic times during my school days when I had a school project to do Dad would ask Professor So-and-So if I could meet with them to get some information.

Yes, I was a university kid but I was always different. As a young child I read a lot but by the time I was thirteen I started to go off books. At school we had to read two books each term, which wasn't a lot really, but when they were really boring, like *Biggles* and the *Famous Five*, well I just gave up and unfortunately have never really regained the taste that I had in those days. The books I always liked the best were biographies, but in those days it wasn't really fashionable to read them. You were supposed to read *The Hobbit* and *Lord of the Rings*, but I tried them and found them a bore.

It's funny what you remember from your early days. Up until the age of five I really didn't have anything eventful in my life. Dad went to work; Mum stayed at home with us and I played. A very different life from that of many of the children I have worked with as a social worker. I was given lots of love and stimulation and at the time I just took it all for granted. It was normal.

When I was about eighteen months old I fell out of my high chair and was concussed. I spent ten days being observed in hospital. I'm not sure whether I can remember the feelings of being separated from my parents, who were only allowed to see me through a glass partition. Right up until I worked in a hospital at the age of twenty-one years old I had a fear of hospitals. When a school friend ended up in a mental hospital after doing his A-levels, I found visiting him such a traumatic experience that I had to go to a pub afterwards.

The next biggest trauma I had was one day when we went to our allotment. I must have been about three years old. I really don't remember anything about the allotment. All I know was that I was riding in the trailer attached to Dad's bike. We didn't have a car until I was eleven years old and so we went everywhere initially on two bikes and then Luke had his own. Edmund must have been on the back of Mum's bike because I was there on my own. Suddenly Dad disappeared. Mum and Luke had gone ahead and I remember shouting, "Where is my Daddy?" He had got a wheel stuck in one of the ruts over the bridge and had gone flying over the handlebars into a pile of nettles.

It sounds funny now but then it was so traumatic. It was only in later years that I knew how lucky I had been.

I often think now that, if a memory like that stays with me forever, what happens to the memories of abused children? It is really frightening to think about.

Yes, I was fortunate to have a good, safe childhood, but I often wish now that I had been more confident. I wish I'd been pushed to join the Brownies or that Mum had persevered with my swimming lessons so that I could swim like a fish like my children can. But then she felt that she was doing the best and I must have worn her down so. In so many ways she has always been a much better mum than me, with a lot more patience and tolerance.

At the time of writing this she is eighty-three years old and is amazing for her age. She is out for hours gardening, cutting the grass. At the start of writing this she was also caring for my father, who was dying of cancer. He died in the early stages of writing the book.

I suppose the only other traumatic thing that happened to me in those early days was when I was bitten on the ear by a dog. My next door neighbours, Wendy and Harry, had a dog called Ricky. I loved Ricky as much as I loved Wendy and Harry. Wendy is the kind of person who just makes you feel completely comfortable. She makes everything, even the most mundane, sound exciting. At least she did to me as a child.

Anyhow, one day I saw who I thought was Ricky at the front of the house and went out to give her a big hug, and then I was bitten on the ear. Apparently she did look just like Ricky. I can remember being totally shocked that she would do such a thing, not my wonderful Ricky.

That experience stayed with me for years, leaving me with a fear of dogs. Unfortunately, I also passed this fear onto my daughter and it took me some time and the experience of a few nice dogs for her to get over it.

We lived in a two-bedroomed house. I slept in with my brothers. I don't remember much about that house. I do, however, remember that there were loads of boys living in our road and, having two brothers myself, they used to come and play in our garden a lot; but then in those days, when cars were a rarity, we used to play in the road too.

We used to play cowboys and Indians, but I always ended up as the Indian and the boys the cowboys. Most of the time I didn't mind though, as I liked wearing my Indian outfit. Dressing up was great fun and I suppose I have never got over it. Those were the days of imaginary games, and falling over and grazing your knee was a traumatic event.

One winter's day when we actually had a decent bit of snow, a rarity in Birmingham, all the kids in the road decided to have a snowball fight, mostly against one of the dads – and guess who got in the way? Me, of course, and someone landed a whopping snowball right in my eye.

In those days I was a right old cry-baby and I suppose I've never changed really, but I try to keep my tears to the traditional adult zone at home. Unfortunately, it doesn't always work, and when I do blub, I feel such a prat.

Going it alone

One day, the time came for me to start school. I lived at number 36 Falconhurst Road, Harborne, Birmingham and I went to St Peter's School. I had been used to going up to school to pick my brothers up and was really looking forward to being at school myself.

I went very happily the first day, but on the second I was a bit reluctant. Not because I didn't want to go – that came many years later – no, it was because during the first day lots of children had cried and I just wanted to get on with some work.

As I write this from my Haven caravan in Wales I remember that most of the teachers in our school came from Wales and we did lots of singing.

I worked hard at school and, having started with no reading or writing skills, by my first Christmas I was able to read some of the Bible Story in church.

Being a church school, we would go to church to celebrate all the Christian festivities. I enjoyed all of this but it never really had a greater meaning as I was brought up with both a father and grandfather who were atheists and a mother who felt that religion had been the cause of many of the ills in the world.

When I was a child they were very much humanists, who believe that it is important to make the most of this life and don't believe in an afterlife. I suppose that I've always kind of been unsure, but over the last decade I have become more interested in more obscure religions.

Anyhow, I enjoyed going to church at primary school and singing *Onward Christian Soldiers* and all of the other gutsy hymns, and I still wow at singing Christmas carols. My dad said that he always liked church music too.

My first best friend at primary school was Helen. When I left to go to senior school I lost touch with her. I have often thought that it would have been nice to be on *Surprise Surprise* and get to meet Helen again through Cilla Black.

She had the most lovely curly blond hair; mine, of course, was dead straight and dark brown. My daughter's hair is just like mine and often I hear her say how she wishes she had nice hair. It is, but she doesn't see it that way.

Helen's dad used to be a rep for Horlicks. She used to have all sorts of products in her house, but then, like now, I hate the smell of Horlicks. Helen remained my friend throughout primary school, although when Heather started at school I had a competitor and sometimes I would be left out of the games.

When I was eight a new girl came to our school. Her name was Emma and I have kept in touch with her ever since. She was a nice girl but not as much fun as Helen. All the boys liked Helen too, and so when we played kiss chase she used to be one of the first girls to be caught.

In those days I liked the twins, Mark and Dan, best. They were in Edmund's class, but one of them was off school very sick for a long time. We never knew what was wrong with him but he was never quite right when he came back to school, and so I think that it was meningitis.

I was never really poorly and sometimes used to be jealous of other children who stayed at home because they were poorly. We had the most wonderful doctor. His name was Dr Jones and he was a black West Indian married to a white woman, most unusual in those days. They had kids but I don't remember ever seeing them.

We used to just turn up at the surgery and queue to see him. Nobody really minded queuing, as he was such a wonderful doctor. I can remember having one of my first jabs and saying that he could do it now and him saying that he'd already done it.

He also believed that you shouldn't keep kids in bed unless they were really poorly and so when Edmund and I had German measles together and couldn't go to school we had a fantastic time playing in the garden. When Dr Jones came to see us we hid from him in the garden. I remember him thinking that it was very funny.

Looking back now, my early childhood days seemed very happy. I loved school but used to get very nervous about returning after the school holidays. Once I was there I was okay – it was just getting there. I had to catch two buses to school, which cost 1 1/2d each.

One day when I went back to school after the holiday I felt really sick and threw up over three adults on the bus – what an embarrassment for my mum and a nuisance for the adults.

I think of children now and how dependent they have become and think of me aged six and my brother aged eight crossing a very busy road and catching these two buses.

On the homeward trek the first bus stop was also used by disabled people going home from a training centre. In those days we called them Spastics but I soon learnt how horrible it was to make fun of them. They seemed all right to me – they just walked and talked a bit funny. I suppose I must have been preparing to be a social worker even in those very early days.

We used to swing around the bus stop and one day I was standing near it when the metal sign fell down, just missing me. My mum was with me at the time and said how lucky I was, as I could have been knocked out.

One day Edmund dropped our bus fare in the charity box. He often threatened to do it and one day he did by mistake. So we had to walk home. By 5.00pm our mum was distraught and sent Luke out on his bike looking for us. We didn't have a phone and so we couldn't ring home. She was so pleased to see us. It was an adventure, but Edmund never dropped the bus fare again.

Ikon

When I was about eight years old my parents, together with some other local people in Birmingham, started Ikon Gallery. The aim was to have somewhere for local artists to exhibit their works. I was brought up with modern art but neither like nor dislike it. What I remember most of those days is folding what seemed like thousands of leaflets for exhibitions and my mum sitting in the first gallery several days a week. Several Ikons on, and it is now an internationally known gallery employing quite a number of staff, but I remember those early days with fond memories.

The second Ikon was in Swallow Street and the building was absolutely filthy. Committee members, their children and we all had to participate in getting it in a decent state for exhibiting. I got bronchitis from all the dust. Years later I would pop in with my teenage friends to eat a bag of chips before we went somewhere else.

My parents have always been humble about what they did but really their perseverance deserves much more acclaim. What I learnt from the Ikon experience was that certain things are worth committing time and perseverance to.

In Summer 2004 Ikon will have a special exhibition celebrating forty years of its existence.

And to comprehensive school

I suppose in lots of ways I have been lucky, riding the waves of misfortune and coming out the other side.

I did well at primary school, took my eleven-plus, which I passed with flying colours, and prepared to start senior school.

Three of my grandparents died before I was ten but I remember President John F. Kennedy's assassination much more than any of their deaths. My parents both cried that day.

I started at Shenley Court School, in Birmingham, in 1967. It was an exciting time to be a teenager – The Beatles were at their peak and mini-skirts were all the rage. I never really wore them because I always felt that my legs were too fat, and I preferred maxis when they came along, but I, along with my cousin, had a Beatles cap.

Starting senior school was exciting and I soon found several boys that I fancied – in particular Peter, but he never fancied me. It wasn't until I was fourteen that I went out with my first boyfriend, another Peter.

I remember my first day at school, it was a scorching hot day and I sat boiled in a cardigan and blazer. I was too shy to ask if I could take them off.

My problem was that I was too introverted and just did what I was told. I never questioned what was expected of me and I used to worry about things that I got wrong. Regularly I would burst into tears in the class. My daughter Phoebe has inherited this trait, although she is a lot more outgoing than I am, and as time goes on is much more able to control it than I was.

Some things that teachers did in those days were horrible. Mr X, the science teacher had this awful habit of getting everyone to stand up and when they answered a question they were allowed to sit down. I used to dread his lessons, which put me off science for life.

The first time the geography teacher met my class he screamed at us saying, "Heads will fly" – that was, if we didn't go into the class quietly. In fact we were a relatively quiet group.

In my professional capacity as a social worker, and as a parent, I have come across teachers who still have this obnoxious approach to their teaching. It's not surprising that so many children, including me, become so fearful of school.

At school there were a few cocky kids. I remember one girl who used to cheek the teachers. At the time I quite admired her and wished that I could be more like her. On one occasion at dinner-time she took a couple of bites out of her doughnut and said that it was rotten and insisted on having another one. She was given another one. I always wished that I had the nerve to do that kind of thing. I think that eventually she was expelled from school and when I was in the midst of having a good time in my late teens she was pushing a baby around Selly Oak, a district of Birmingham.

Chapter 2 – Lessons in Life

School phobia

I suspect that most readers have a phobia about something: mine was school.

One day when I was fourteen years old I found that I just couldn't go to school. It wasn't that I didn't want to go; I just couldn't. To this day I still don't know why I couldn't go, but what it did was introduce me to the world of social work, which I would enter eleven years later as a professional.

Social workers talked a lot about empathy when I qualified in 1982, but empathy doesn't get close to what it actually feels like. When your deputy headteacher cries in your kitchen because she can't get you to school, you really wonder what life is about.

School phobia pushed me towards a world I probably wouldn't have even considered before. I was the child of a university family. We just didn't do social work. We gave to charity and supported all sorts of campaigns, but to actually work with the most disadvantaged and unwanted people in society, well, we didn't do that.

This is, of course, a cynical comment but what I have found in my lifetime is the snobbery between different groups of people in society, and what I found very early on, and have continued through my life to find, is that I am a misfit who fits everywhere and nowhere.

What school phobia taught me was to observe and be interested in people, all sorts of people. What it did for me academically was to make me unfit for the traditional academic world. I missed out on education at the crucial point of my school days. I scraped through the relevant O-levels and failed the A-levels.

It also changed my personality from an introvert to an exotic extrovert. My house was the place to be and I had loads of male friends. I wasn't promiscuous – in fact, I am probably a strange product of my time, as from the ages of seventeen to forty-seven I only had two men in my life.

Although my formal education went astray, I received a much more intensive form of education whilst being treated by the professionals. No one could get me back to school but because I was a middle-class university kid there wasn't the possibility of involving a social worker. I did have contact with the Wag Man (Education Welfare Officer) but he worked very co-operatively with my parents and the school and I was dealt with very discreetly. I suppose it was a little embarrassing for the school when my father had nominated the headteacher as a governor to the university, and my granddad was a governor too.

At the same time as my having school phobia my brother Luke was out in India doing the hippy trail. That was the times – it was 1969.

School phobia gave me a personal insight to my introversion and how disabling it becomes. It is now over thirty years since I got through my school phobia and yet I can reincarnate those feelings in an instant. I feel that this has made me incredibly sensitive to people who have suffered in all sorts of ways. I will never know exactly how they feel but what I do know is that they have to make a choice about whether they want to survive and head towards a happier, more fulfilling life or whether they want to give in to what has badly damaged their life. My role is to help them head towards that happier life, not by doing it for them but by helping them walk along that prickly path and by removing the brambles which may damage them along the way.

It is hard to tell you what it actually felt like, but I can remember the phone ringing and going to hide in case anyone wanted to talk to me.

I remember getting dressed for school and walking halfway to school with my dad, getting panicky and returning home to a disappointed mother. I remember locking myself in the toilet, having hysterics, and my dad threatening to take the hinges off the door to get me out. I also remember being taken to see a psychiatrist who was German and who gave me lots of pathetically simple tests. I know now that she was probably testing my IQ, but at the time I just found it so incredibly humiliating.

All of these feelings I have taken on board and nowadays if I visit a professional with a distressed child I squirm at some of the tests, looks and comments that are made, remembering what they felt like to me.

It's funny the names you remember and those you don't, and whether going through the experience and the deep feelings that you will never see the light of day again may block those names.

The doctor who helped bring back my daylight was a psychologist, who later became one of the university doctors. I wouldn't go to the first appointment and was fortunate that he was persuaded to come and visit me at home. He came, we talked and I agreed to go with Mum to see him. I visited him several times and each time he introduced a form of behaviour therapy.

The first time we went by car, then we went together by bus and then I went by bus on my own. I can remember screaming at him that I hated him and he told me that he now knew that I was on the mend. Whatever he meant by that.

I got to like going there to see him and talk to him, but I never got back to school.

One Friday I was asked to come and speak to the Wag Man, who came to our house. He told me that I had no choice and that on Monday I had to go back to school otherwise I would go to live in a children's home until I was eighteen years old. I can feel the same panic as I write this as I did then. I had no choice. I know now that it was a prearranged ploy to get me back to school and that they had no intention or power to implement it, but at the time it was just awful.

Well, I went to school on the Monday and remember going into a triple lesson of chemistry, a subject I hated, and being asked by the teacher whether I wanted to do it for O-level. When I said no, he said that I needn't bother much with it then.

I think now of children who manage to return to school after not going for a long time for all sorts of reasons, and wonder what the teachers say to them.

No one expected me to do well in my O-levels, and in fact for Spanish (which I had only completed one term before returning) and biology I was put in the CSE group. I scraped through 5 O-levels and got Grade 1 for Spanish and Grade 2 for biology, so I much exceeded expectations.

Moving on

The problem with suffering from a phobia is that you become so hypersensitive that at times you feel that it will come back and you won't be able to cope again. Even to this day there are short times in my life where I feel that I cannot cope and then a day later I bounce back again.

As I go through these feelings I tend to have an emotional battle with myself. My logical side says "What are you fussing about?" and my panicky side says "I will never get through this."

I have learnt through my brother that we all go through a number of mood states all the time and each of these states have a beginning and an ending. This has helped me when I have felt very low.

Getting back to school was an easy and a difficult problem. It was easy because I just went, but I often found that I couldn't cope in lessons and went crying to my form teacher, Miss W. Interestingly enough, her subject was needlework, which I was always hopeless at, but she was really good to me. She gave me the confidence to carry on.

I was in the third year at senior school and I was out of school from the October half term until after the Easter holidays. I eventually stayed on till the sixth form and so I am very grateful to the staff at Shenley Court School for their support.

School phobia really set me off in the direction of being a misfit. Everyone in my family achieved well academically, but strangely neither me, Luke nor Edmund followed the expected traditional university path. Edmund is now a Buddhist monk and I believe that Luke is still searching for his true role in life and, like many people, may not feel totally settled until he can find it.

I recently told a couple of service users about my school phobia and they were amazed that I had got such a good job. I wanted to say that it was because I had such good parents and support, but didn't. I just thought that I couldn't be their parents but I could try to help them to get the best for them, and whether I did only time will tell.

The extrovert

Having been a little mouse, I suddenly found a great deal of confidence and found myself a popular person. I had my own fashion, which was more of a hippy style and which was copied by my friends. I had the purple suede jacket, which I kept for fun and which looks great as a dress on Phoebe.

I went to loads of discos and parties and had lots of friends. Sometimes I would spend time with female friends and on other occasions spend time with my hippy male friends. I had two friends in particular who I would walk to school with and spend time with. These were Brian and Tom. I lost touch with them many years ago and have often wondered what happened to them.

Life was a round of school and parties. My parents had enough money to give me pocket money and so I didn't get a Saturday or holiday job. I once got paid 50p for washing up for the local cricket club with my friend Angie. She had youngish parents and I was always jealous of the fact. My Mum was thirty-five when she had me and – guess what – yes, I was thirty-five when I had Phoebe.

Yes, life was fun and easy. All I had to do was try and keep up with my homework. In those days I was also very slim. I had hipbones and an indented tummy, which I am very jealous of now.

Phoebe is podgier than me but still looks quite good in fashionable clothes, which, at the age of twelve, she is keen to wear. She is careful not to be extravagant in her choice, the same as I was then.

Yes, I had the body, so I could flaunt it. I always thought I had fat legs but no one ever really remarked on them. I know now that whatever I looked like, if I was supposed to meet the man of my dreams then I would, but then being slim was so important. I look now at the huge size of some of Phoebe's friends and wonder why their parents have let them become so large.

I was extrovert, full of life, and yet through my school phobia experience I became a great deal wiser than many of my peers.

Just missing Slade

My first real boyfriend was called Pete. I was nearly fifteen and he was seventeen. He was tall, slim, blond and wore glasses. We went out together for about three months and then I dumped him.

I had gone on a school exchange to France and came back realising that it was more fun to flirt with a lot of boys. Of course, the French boy who I fancied wasn't interested in me and picked a girl who I thought was rather unpopular, but then I was only disappointed for five minutes.

Lots of my friends seemed to have boyfriends for two minutes and then they either went out with a gang of girls or found a new one. I tended either to have no one or a long relationship, which has been the pattern of my life.

Pete was a nice bloke, although I found him a little boring, but what I do regret is that I never got to see Slade at his school. A few months later they became famous and tickets were out of our price range.

Slim and blond

When I think of Chris, my second boyfriend, he was blond with very straight, soft hair. He was a little bit taller than my five feet four inches. I went out with Chris for nine months, a long time in those days. He was six months older than me. I'm not really sure where we met or how we started going out, but I enjoyed my time with Chris. My mum also really liked him, which these days probably wouldn't be that cool, but then it seemed okay.

However, Chris was probably the ruination of my skinny figure as he introduced me to the delights of home-made chips. My mother was a healthy-eating parent and so chips to us were a treat served up when we went to a restaurant. While my parents savoured Chinese or Indian food, I would have fish, chips and peas.

The demise of Chris came when I fancied my next boyfriend. Little did I know at the time that from the age of seventeen to forty-five I would only have one man in my love life.

Tim

I can only introduce Tim to the reader, as he would be around in my life for the next twenty-nine years. We were seen as the ideal couple, devoted to each other.

Tim became one of the gang that used to frequent my house and in fact was a good friend of Chris. I never cheated on Chris – that is just something I wouldn't do – but I was attracted to Tim. One of those animal/chemical mating things.

Tim lived in a big house in another part of Birmingham. He had an elder brother, who in those days had long hair and looked like John Lennon, and a younger sister who remains like a sister to me today.

Tim was clever but dyslexic. He could read a technical manual and create from it. He became a computer professional and was very good at what he did. He was much quieter than me and took time to get to know people. He was also, in lots of ways, a hopeless communicator.

I had that amazing feeling with Tim, which was being lovesick. If you have been lovesick, you will know what it feels like; if not, maybe you will some day.

Tim was around for a long time. We married when I was thirty-one and produced three children, so his tale will permeate through a lot of the future years.

On my forty-fifth birthday Tim arrived late at night at the house where I then lived with the children. I had been out for the evening with the children. It was pouring with rain outside and suddenly there was a knock on Joshua's bedroom window (we lived in a bungalow). It was Tim, and from that day I knew that it was the real end of our life together. Two years on from that day and I think sadly about Tim, someone who for so long was such a part of my life and who will probably through his endeavours make the publishing of this book possible.

Only a wife and mother

I liked my deputy head, who also taught me Spanish, but he was such a male chauvinist pig. When I was choosing my A-levels Mr

L said that it didn't matter whether I did three A-levels or not as I would probably just stay at home as a housewife and mother. How wrong he was, as I have never stayed at home other than for my maternity leave or working around the school holidays. I hadn't a clue what to do when I left school, but getting married and having children was not in my plans at all. I was having too good a time.

Being in the sixth form was great and a round of parties. We were a close group, with some slight revolutionary tendencies. At our last assembly me and at least a dozen members of our group suddenly played the Monty Python signature tune on the then popular kazoos. Mr L, who was in charge that day, seemed sufficiently cross to lecture to us as the offending group, but surely he must have found it funny.

I have never really been a sporty person and so when I got the opportunity of doing some voluntary work instead of games I jumped at it. I used to go one morning a week to Victoria School, which, when I started there, catered for physically disabled children.

I helped generally in the class, doing whatever the teacher asked of me. Little did I realise at the time that by doing this voluntary work I was investing in my own future. I just enjoyed going there and began to think that I would like to do something like working at the school for a living.

I left school with GCEs, failing both my French and history A-levels, and wondered what was next. Coming from a pretty academic family I felt as if I was the "thicko", a feeling that has never left me.

Chapter 3 – A Naïve Worker

What a tragic start to a working life

It is hard to write about my first experience of work, not because of the job I did but because of the tragic circumstances that I started my working life in. I started working in Birmingham city centre as a saleslady in the minor electrics department of Debenhams. In other words, I sold toasters, irons and Teasmaids (which were all the rage at the time).

I learnt fairly quickly what to do and was good with using the till and doing credit cards, but absolutely useless at putting things back in boxes when customers had had a look at them. I am still useless at getting things into boxes or folding letters to fit into envelopes. Stephen gets frustrated with me when I find it impossible to fold a letter into three parts and get one into an envelope with a window... well, I just give up and play the pathetic damsel in distress.

I found the work extremely tiring and I never knew how much your feet and legs could ache from standing on them all day. I started the same day as another woman. We were both temporary Christmas workers and when I started the job I knew that I had another job to go to the following January.

It was early November 1974, a month that stayed in the memory of many Brummies for years afterwards as it was the month of the Birmingham pub bombings. In fact, I had only been working in Debenhams for a short time when it happened.

I remember the day vividly because I answered the telephone to an upset aunty from Bristol asking if we were all okay. I told her that of course we were and she realised that I didn't know and asked if I had seen the news that night. I said that I hadn't, none of us had because we were too busy.

She then told me about the bombs and where they were and how many people had been killed. I immediately got off the phone and told my parents. We watched the news and saw policemen crying as they went to a scene of devastation. I remember feeling extremely panicky, wondering what had happened to my world and wondering if Tim was safe. He used to go occasionally to one of the pubs after an evening class that he attended.

We didn't dare ring his parents in case he wasn't okay and so the wait to hear was unbearable. I often think how tormenting it must be for people not to know whether their missing relatives are alive or dead.

The next morning I had to catch the bus into the city centre as usual and walk near the scene of devastation, wondering if any of my work colleagues had been killed. I remember the solemnity of the occasion. Some people didn't come into work – they couldn't face it – but then the bosses didn't know whether they were alive or dead. It wasn't only the sight itself; it was the smell of the air. It reeked of roast pork. A fireman friend had told me some years before that he could never eat pork as it smelt just like human flesh, and now we were having this experience. That smell stayed in our memories for days, as Birmingham city centre is fairly small, and I can even remember it now.

We learnt that there had been a hen party held in one of the pubs that night, with staff from Lewis's, and they were believed all to be dead.

This was an experience that my generation had not come across before. It left us in fear and whenever we heard a siren we wondered whether another bomb had gone off.

The other impact was that, although it was near to Christmas, shoppers just stopped coming into the city centre. My days were long and boring. It was only working with a nice colleague that helped me through the time.

We also got the false alarms from idiots who thought it was funny but who caused a great deal of distress, and had to empty the shop.

I must have been okay at what I did because I was offered a permanent job. I, however, had the first real job of my own choosing to go to, starting in the January.

Woodgate Valley Day Nursery

I started at the nursery on 6th January 1975 as a junior nursery assistant. I have lost count of the times that I have written down this information for job applications.

Woodgate Valley was a new housing estate where people had been moved from the Birmingham slums. The nursery was purpose-built and was attached to the day centre. The aim of the nursery was to provide local working people with quality childcare.

The community centre was a church-based centre made up of several Christian denominations. It was, in its time, a rather progressive project but to me it was just normal. It is only in later years that I realised that it was progressive.

My job was to work with the young children. There were two junior nursery assistants and we earned the princely sum of £600 a year. I worked from 8.00am to 4.00pm and the other junior worked from 10.00am to 6.00pm. There were other staff but, except for the manager and deputy, they worked part-time.

It's funny the things you remember about jobs. I remember things like the poor ventilation in the toilet for changing smelly bottoms. I also remember when we had several children with suspected meningitis and we had to keep them isolated.

Looking after the children was fine, but after doing this for a few months I began to get bored. I wanted a new challenge.

One day I came home from work and found Mum looking

through the local paper. She saw an advert for an occupational therapy (OT) aide, working at a geriatric hospital (the terminology used in those days). Neither of us really knew what the job was but it sounded a little different. I applied for but decided not to tell the manager at the nursery unless I got the job. I was going to skive the day off work (a practice I can honestly say that I have never done because I have always had a guilt complex and thought that the chances are that I would see someone that I knew) but, in fact, the day before the interview I went to work and the mother of one of the nursery children said that I shouldn't be there because I had conjunctivitis. She was a nurse specialising in eye-care. I therefore went along secretively to the interview the following day. When I think of it now I think that it was a bit ironic going to an interview at a hospital when I was off sick.

I got the job and a few days later gave in my notice.

Daisy, Daisy

I worked half-time in the OT department at West Heath Hospital in Birmingham for a period of eight months. Part of my time was spent visiting the wards and the rest of the time was in the day hospital.

There were three OT aides. One had been there for a long time; the other started at roughly the same time as me.

Having previously worked in a nursery, and on occasions chasing lively kids around the housing estate, I now found myself having to slow down dramatically. Some of the older people who I worked with suffered from Parkinson's disease and would get stuck going through doorways.

I had to be incredibly patient and would sometimes think to myself, "Oh, come on," but would always be outwardly pleasant. This is a skill that I have developed for most of my career. You have to be outwardly pleasant both with your clients and your colleagues, otherwise your effectiveness diminishes dramatically.

Anyhow, as with all of my jobs, I learnt a lot in a relatively short time. I can still today, nearly thirty years later, remember practical things like how to put a coat on someone who has little use in one of their arms from having a stroke. My mother used to laugh when I would sing a nursery rhyme followed by "Daisy" or "It's a Long Way to Tipperary".

My love of working with different types and ages of people started here.

Hard reality

Not everything was rosy. There were a lot of young elderly people living in the hospital, who were only in their mid-seventies. Some of them had lived there for several years and had become extremely institutionalised.

It was often felt that, if patients didn't go home from the wards quickly, they would never go home. Of course, we now have community care, but sometimes I think that, although the conditions were pretty poor, for some people the sense of friendship both amongst the elderly people and from the staff was better than living alone at home and looking forward to the homecare visit each day.

The conditions on the wards were also not what you would hope for. There was a shortage of clothing for the patients and so many would sit all day in their nighties, often without a dressing gown to give them a degree of dignity.

There was a shortage of nursing staff and so often patients would ask me if I could get them a nurse because they were desperate for the toilet but after lengthy periods of time they still hadn't been attended to, and I was frustrated as I was not allowed to help them.

Some patients didn't bother asking and nurses were confronted with smelly urine puddles and soaking wet nighties. The nurses, through their own frustration, were not always as patient as you would hope them to be.

Older people who were still "with it" were in the same ward as older people who lived in a world of their own. To some of these people I would become a mother, daughter or other friend or relative trapped in their memories.

Some had ritualistic practices, which to me as a twenty-one-year-old seemed rather bizarre, such as the woman who fanatically used her urine-soaked nightie to clean a table in front of her. She seemed very happy in her own world and to this day I wonder which is best, letting people live happily in a fantasy world or them being frustrated and confused in the real world. In Part II, if you read Bob's story, you will see a dramatised version of these ideas.

Many of these older people were lonely and desperate for any break from the routine. They looked forward to the exercise sessions run by me and my colleagues, and to the chat, which we would bring with us for our hourly visit.

The flu

How many people say that they have the flu when they have a bad cold? Well, I had the flu. I remember it starting with an extremely bad headache, arriving home and being violently sick just as I walked through the front door.

I lived with my parents in a three-bedroomed flat near to where we used to live. My grandfather had died and left my parents some money, enough to buy their dream house near the Shropshire Union Canal in Gnosall.

They felt guilty about having two houses when there were only the three of us at home and so they had tried to rent a flat, but found some difficulties finding one and so had bought one instead.

I got the flu and was off work for two weeks. Actually, the second week was holiday but I was really still getting over the flu. When I returned to work, about ten older people had died, including four who I had become quite attached to.

I am, deep down, an eccentric and just love talking to all sorts of people, and so as well as talking to my OT and physio colleagues I enjoyed talking to the ambulance drivers, who worked both on the 999 calls and the regular journeys taking older people between hospital and their homes.

I had some very interesting discussions, including advice on how to commit suicide sensitively. I was told to take a bottle of booze and some pills rather than jump off a high-rise building, as it made less mess for the ambulance men to clear up. A sobering thought for anyone.

Whilst I was working at West Heath Hospital I began to explore the idea of becoming a social worker. I had vaguely thought about it for a number of years but didn't know any social workers or know how to become one.

I wrote to the Council for Education and Training in Social Work (CCETSW) and told them what I had done and asked what I should do next. They suggested that I try to work with handicapped children. (In 1976 the term "disabled" was seen as negative, the reverse to today.)

The Titanic and the murderer

During my working life I have come across some extremely interesting people and have a lot of stories to tell. As a child I was very taken by Somerset Maugham short stories about the different characters that he met on his travels.

I suppose my first really sensational characters who are worthy of recounting were a man who had been a cabin boy on the *Titanic*, and a murderer.

I met the former when I became a Young Birmingham Volunteer. I had been given the task of working with the Youth Co-ordinator on a community newspaper and during our trawl of stories we came across the man with his *Titanic* tale to tell. He lived in a multi-storey flat in Birmingham. I remember being fascinated by his tale. He said that people just couldn't believe that the *Titanic* was sinking.

Unfortunately the Youth Co-ordinator had rather too much of a crush on me, which made life rather difficult, and so I stopped doing this voluntary work.

My murderer is a very different tale. I was doing some voluntary work at a club for people who were then called "maladjusted". In my working career there have been so many different terminologies.

My role as a volunteer was just to chat with people who attended the club, which was held in a hospital. Some of the people who attended the club lived in the hospital; others lived in the community and came along to the club.

One day I was talking to a man who seemed to be on his own. We started chatting about all sorts of things and then after about ten minutes he started to tell me why he came along to the club. He told me that he had murdered a relative and that part of his treatment was to come along to the club.

At the time I wasn't sure whether to believe him or not, as in previous visits I had heard some fascinating stories that had turned out to be fantasies. However, on this occasion it was true. Apparently the Volunteer Co-ordinator and a nurse had been watching us closely. I had been aware of being watched and had wondered whether I was doing something wrong. They told me later that they were just checking that I was okay. On subsequent visits I was allowed to talk to this man but I was always watched to make sure that I was okay and had to leave at a different time from the man.

To this day, I never quite know how I feel about these

conversations and have never sought to work with people who are mentally ill.

Chapter 4 –
Being Somewhere at the Right Time

The effects of my school phobia in terms of my academic belief in myself have stayed with me, and probably will do forever, but what has also developed is my belief in being somewhere at the right time.

When I received the letter from someone at CCETSW suggesting that I should work with handicapped children, I wondered how could I do this and I wrote to the headteacher at Victoria School where I had volunteered when I was at school, asking for his advice.

He wrote back, asking me to come in for a chat. Little did I know at the time that the school was expanding dramatically and that he was to offer me a job. He wanted me to work as a welfare assistant in a new department, which was to be called "Planned Dependence".

I loved working at Victoria School and would have stayed there for many years had Tim not gone to university in York and had I not decided to try to go and live there with him.

I learnt a great deal from this job, about how to work with disabled children, about working in teams and about looking for the best in children. I loved going there every day and was given a high level of responsibility, which I enjoyed.

If You're Happy and You Know It, Clap Your Hands

Working at Victoria School was particularly important to me. I was treated as a valued member of staff and was given the opportunity to develop skills to benefit the children I was working with. I worked with disabled children and knew why they were disabled and I shared in the frustration of the unknown.

Little did I know that nearly fifteen years later I would go through some of the loss and pain that many of their parents were going through, with the death of my own baby daughter.

There were happy and sad times at Victoria School. Christmas was brilliant, as all children and staff had the full works of a brilliantly cooked turkey dinner, with alternatives for vegetarians. In those days there was little knowledge of ethnic foods.

As members of staff we shared looking after the children and having our Christmas dinner. We started in the staff room with a glass of sherry, had dinner with wine and returned to the staff room for liqueurs. When I think of it now, how those of us who had to change nappies managed, I really don't know. I walked to work so the drinks didn't affect me.

I learnt a lot at Victoria School and there were some children who had a lasting effect on me, just because of who they were. My favourite child was an Asian boy called Raj. It is hard to explain, but he was about nine years old and was regarded as not being able to communicate, but he always seemed so happy and had a look of complete serenity on his face. I would touch his hand or his face or tickle him and he would look at me with this most amazing look and the most beautiful eyes. I often wonder now if Raj's condition was what Buddhists try to achieve but through a world of intellect.

I remember other children but not their names and often wonder whether they are still alive or what happened to them. In times of complete self-centredness I have often thought of these children and their lack of future and that it is so important to do something useful with my life in homage to them and what they taught me.

There were two brothers who were wheelchair-bound, both suffering from muscular dystrophy, which meant, in those days, that to live till the age of eighteen would be an unusual event. I remember having several discussions with the younger brother, who was very mentally alert about what he would go through. He said that he was going to die like his brother would and that there was nothing he could do about it. He was quite calm and amazingly wise for his twelve years when he talked about this. At the time it just seemed the right thing to do. I wasn't upset or embarrassed; I just wanted to be with him to listen to what he had to say. He was important. Thinking on this now, this is how I feel about all the people I work with. At that time they were the most important people in the world. Of course, this then leads to difficulties when I consider my children and Stephen and other people who are important in my personal life.

I have been fortunate, through misfortune, to be able to find a soulmate who understands why I need to write this book and tell these tales.

Paul was another happy soul. He was about thirteen years old and was a biggish boy. I often found that the children who were wheelchair-bound were either painfully thin through wasting diseases or rather too heavy.

Paul was disabled because as a young child he had fallen through the glass in a relative's greenhouse. Until then he had been just a "normal" child.

On a few occasions my mum came to help with taking the children on some trips. She particularly took to Paul and learnt through him all the words and actions to "If You're Happy and You Know It". She used to say how much she enjoyed his happiness.

Very recently mum mentioned, out of the blue, a time when she had come with the children and me on a trip to Birmingham city centre. I remember that one of the brothers was very excited. He said that he had never been there before. I remember thinking how awful to reach this age (fourteen) and to have never been to town before. There were, and still are, so many things that so many of us just take for granted.

It also makes me think of my own dad when he had been housebound for about six weeks and we managed to get him into my car to take him out for a ride. I suddenly saw a whole refreshed world through my dad's eyes – the beauty of the trees and the renewed excitement of his passion for canal boats.

Victoria School was about being somewhere at the right time, an experience which has happened to me several times in my life. Whilst I was there some members of staff got interested in the work of Professor Peto from Hungary and his development of "conductive education". They decided to have a go and I happened to be working in the nursery at the time where the first bits of conductive education were undertaken in potty training. Children with cerebral palsy who went from extremes of floppiness to stiffness within a short period of time had much more control over their bodies.

One day I told Mr J, the headteacher, that I was thinking about being a social worker. He was initially concerned, but was glad that I was getting lots of hands-on experience before I went and did some training.

His experience of social workers, he told me, was not very good. This was also shared by the physios, who I worked closely with. One of them told me that on one occasion she gave a social worker a great deal of detail about why a certain child would never walk again. She said that at the end of the explanation the social worker had asked when she could tell the parents that the child would walk. I sympathised with her greatly when she said that she felt like tearing her hair out.

Although I am an advocate of better relations between social work and the media, this doesn't mean that I believe that all social workers are good at what they do. They are not. I have known some awful and some brilliant social workers in my time.

Most of my days at Victoria School were happy but there were times when I became frustrated or embarrassed, not by what the kids did, but by myself. I remember one such time extremely vividly – it was the day I caused the fire alarm to go off.

When it was bad weather, we would have a teacher and a welfare assistant on playground duty. Well, this particular day I was the welfare assistant and my teacher failed to turn up. I had two hyperactive children to keep an eye on, which was okay, but then another child had a fit. I was following all the correct procedures and then one of the hyperactive kids decided to hit the fire alarm button. Suddenly staff appeared from everywhere and the school was emptied in record time. I had to tell the head what had happened. He said it was the best practice he had ever had – because it was snowing outside everyone took it seriously.

I could have stayed at Victoria School for many years. I was very happy there, but at twenty-two years old I was ready for the next adventure in my life.

Chapter 5 – Life's Lessons

Cold and hopeless

Tim applied and got into university in York to do psychology. I decided to move to York and try to get a job. He went in October 1977. I left Victoria School at Christmas 1977 and moved up to York.

Tim was living in digs in a big, but very cold, house and I crept in to stay with him. I went to the Job Centre to try to get a job but was told that the chances of me getting anything were very small. After a week I felt defeated and went and stayed for a few days in Sheffield with my pretend adopted sister Kim.

She and her family seemed so happy and I felt so miserable. I can remember watching *Newsnight* and then going to bed wondering whether I would be happy again.

I returned to Birmingham and my parents, feeling defeatist, and leaving Tim to his new exciting life in York.

The dole queue

I signed on and started applying for jobs. My confidence was bashed. My boyfriend was having a fab time in York and as far as I was concerned I had failed. I am someone who gets disheartened but also bounces back. The only good thing about being miserable for me is that I tend to lose weight.

A lot of my friends had, by now, dispersed around the country and I, having little money, stayed in a lot. I applied and applied and applied for jobs, but I was too clever for some and not clever enough or experienced enough for others.

I have said for many years now that I would love to be in charge of finding the people within Social Services with the ideas and helping them to bring those ideas to fruition. I find that as a society we are not good enough at encouraging each other. Why can't some wacky ideas work?

Anyone who has applied for lots of jobs knows what a soul-destroying experience it is, but I was fortunate because my parents were still there to back me up. They didn't want me moping around and so I went and did some voluntary work.

Part of my week I went on the children's ward at the local hospital and helped the teacher. The other part of the week I volunteered at St Basil's Centre, a project for homeless young people in Birmingham. I didn't know at the time but St Basil's would yet again give me a lucky break and lead me in a new direction. The children were there mainly due to accidents, although there were a few with life-threatening diseases.

Brown Girl in the Ring

One day I got a job again. It was a temporary job, providing maternity cover, working as a playleader for Birmingham Friendship Housing Association on a latchkey scheme.

Remember that I worked in Birmingham, a city which is known for being progressive, and was leading in play. My job was to go to the city centre, a big old house in Tyseley, where I would meet the children. I would then take them to school in a minibus and pick them up in the evening. We also ran a playgroup. During the holidays we had the children all day. I had to shop for the food, etc. When I arrived the worker who was going on maternity leave overlapped with me for a short time so she could show me the ropes.

It's funny, odd things that you remember. The permanent worker used to wash all the tea towels in bleach. I thought, I'm not having that, and one of the first things I bought was the biggest box of Persil that I could find.

I loved driving the kids to school and meeting them. They would come out of school all excited to show me what they had made, drawn, etc.

The minibus wasn't much good though, and one day it broke down with two more children to take to school. I didn't have enough money on me for the bus fare to take the kids to school and so walked with them to the local police station and asked if I could borrow the bus fare. A friendly Bobby took it out of his own pocket and gave it to me. Imagine the number of forms he would have to fill in today. He got it back, of course, and the minibus was fixed.

We used to sing in the minibus and one of the favourite songs was "Brown Girl in the Ring". Many of the kids had black parents and they seemed to identify with the song. As a Brummie, even though I had been brought up in a white area, I was used to having lots of black people around.

I have mixed memories about this job. In some ways it was good; in others it was limited and at times boring. It was also tiring. I had to be at work at 7.30am and didn't leave until 6.00pm. I could go home during the day but it was quite a journey from Tyseley back to Bournville. If I stayed I was bored, if I went home I snoozed. I have always loved afternoon naps and as well as my current interests and my lifelong membership of the Orange Squash Society (I don't drink tea or coffee and am regularly discriminated against at conferences I attend – hint, nod, wink). I would be happy to write *Snooze*, the monthly comic for nappers.

Not everything was so innocent. One day I was waiting to pick up a child from one of the schools and chatted with one of the waiting parents. She told me how a man had walked into the school, assaulted a young child and left her crying. She had apparently walked past two teachers' classrooms crying and had gone home in a distressed state.

This incident had put all the local schools on alert and made life more difficult for me because it was not possible to get to three schools at the same time. The worst of the schools was the Catholic school. If you weren't there exactly on time they would kick up a real fuss, which meant that another school would have to wait to look after the kids. I always had to praise them for their support.

One icy morning I left home and drove my usual route. A big black van was parked and I went into the back of it. I wrote the minibus off and then my boss found that the insurance was only for drivers aged twenty-five plus. I was twenty-two. What a lucky break, though: I was okay, just a bit shocked, and the police laid the blame on the van for being parked badly and with dirty reflectors. My boss was pleased that at last she could now get a decent new minibus.

I left in the December at the end of my six months and signed on yet again.

My first direct experience of the media was a couple of weeks after I had started working at Tyseley. I was filmed walking out of the centre to the minibus with my colleague for a documentary about latchkey schemes. We had to walk out twice and pretend to look natural. It seemed such a hoot at the time.

Homeless and rootless

I have been fortunate never to be homeless or rootless. I went back to work as a volunteer for St Basil's Centre in January 1978, and in March 1978 I got a half-time job working as a youth leader in the advice centre.

When I started it was a small kiosk in the Bull Ring shopping centre and then they got a coffee bar and much bigger premises near the law courts. We worked with young people aged between sixteen and twenty-five who turned up in Birmingham with nowhere to stay. Most of them stayed firstly at the night shelter, which was nicknamed "The Boot" and then some would find more permanent accommodation.

The thought of going it alone at the age of sixteen is awful to me. Many of the young people had had brushes with the law. They would spend their Giros on booze and then come begging for food for the rest of the week. They often sat in the coffee bar all day because they had nothing else to do. Some days we would just get a couple of young people, other days the place would be packed.

Our role was to give advice and general support. We would encourage young people to look for jobs, but at that time it was hard getting work in Birmingham anyhow, but even more difficult for young people who had little or no qualifications and, in many cases, criminal records. I made a friend who I still keep in touch with, called Sue. She was in charge of the advice centre.

I left St Basil's with a bit of a bad taste in September 1980 when I went to college. I had applied to Westhill College to do community and youth work. Having failed once, when I was twenty-one, to get anywhere with social work training, someone mentioned to me about community and youth work training, and the philosophy behind the training seemed more in line with my thinking.

I applied in 1978 to go to Westhill but was told to get some more experience first. In 1979 I applied again and asked the boss at St Basil's if he would give me a reference. Well, when I got to the interview Westhill asked me if I knew about my strange reference, which neither recommended me for the course nor didn't. I said that I knew nothing about it. I later spoke to my boss about it. She was very angry and asked the big boss about it.

As workers we all had an independent consultant to talk with on a regular basis about our work, and mine had been a close friend of the boss. She was extremely angry when she heard what he had said, and she challenged him about it. She was never happy with his answer and I think it tainted their friendship a little.

At the time it was like being punched in the stomach and not knowing why. I got into college anyway and found out later that he had done nasties on other people too.

I hate the abuse of personal power and could never do this to anyone. People should be given a second chance or receive an explanation of why this isn't appropriate.

I have a close friend who has been in dispute with her boss for over a year. She works for a TV company. Her boss has questioned her competency but refuses to outline what it is that she is unable to do. I find this so unfair – how can we ever get better at things if we don't know what we are doing wrong, and why should someone like her boss be so cowardly in not telling her the truth about what he feels that she cannot do? I don't think that I will ever understand this kind of cruelty.

Chapter 6 – A Slow Entry

My course was interesting but I suppose my school phobia and lack of confidence in my own academic ability began to re-emerge.

I got through it though. My two placements were okay but not particularly inspiring and still today I feel miffed about the lucky students who get the ace placements and those who have to be creative but don't get the acclaim for their creativity.

I finished in 1982 with two qualifications: a Certificate in Community and Youth Work and a CQSW (Certificate of Qualification in Social Work).

I wanted to be a neighbourhood worker and applied for any jobs I could see around the Midlands. I had a two-day interview for a job in Nottingham, which was one of my worst experiences and would certainly put me off ever applying to go into the *Big Brother* house.

The first night we sat having a formal dinner and were supposed to just join in with the interviewing panel. We didn't know whether we should say a little or a lot. Most of the panel were local women living on the estate, and getting any conversation started with them was hard going. We were told that in the morning only half of us would be interviewed for the job and so we had to spend a restless night wondering whether we would be interviewed or not, and whether we wanted it or not.

When, next morning, I was not one of those chosen I was disappointed for about two minutes and then celebrated my release from the torment, most probably with an ice cream. Ice cream is my downfall – I love it. I wouldn't say I was an ice-aholic, but I sure love it.

Death of a Cadbury

For my last few years in Birmingham I was an active Liberal Democrat. I didn't care what fun Labour supporters made of me and when I was at college one of the lecturers was an active Conservative supporter. The Liberal Democrats were who I was happy with.

In the midst of my job-hunting Jocelyn Cadbury, the MP for Northfield, killed himself. For those of you who are not Brummies, you are probably unaware of how important the Cadbury family were, and may still be today.

When I was at college some students were asked to help wait at the Lord Mayor's dinner, which was seen as a great honour. I remember seeing the guest list, which had all sorts of people on it, but there was also a section that said "The Cadbury Family".

Jocelyn Cadbury had shot himself in his mother's garden after a failed love affair. This led to a by-election. Jocelyn had been a Conservative but most of the family, through their Quaker roots, were Liberals. This left the family in a quandary, as they were pulled between family loyalty and politics. They decided not to actively support any of the candidates. All of this was told to me at the time.

So Jamie, the Liberal Democrat candidate, who became a friend of mine, was supported by the by-election team. I spent six weeks working on the by-election and it was one of the most exciting, enjoyable experiences of my life.

My main job was to write back to people and help them solve individual difficulties (the case work). I got to meet some of the then Liberal Democrat bigwigs, and became a regular occupant with Jamie on the Battle Bus.

My favourite Lib Dem celebrity was David Penhaligon. He sat with me on the floor at the campaign headquarters, writing back to people. He was a very warm, down-to-earth person, who told me that MPs were only the puppets of the Civil Service. How different life might be now if he hadn't been killed in a car crash and instead had perhaps become leader of the Liberal Democrats.

He also bought me a meal. Everyone was going for a curry and I said that I wasn't going. When he asked why and I said that I couldn't afford it, he said that he'd pay for me as long as I let him have a go at driving my Mini (Tim and I shared a Mini). He said that he used to have one and fancied having a go again; he even repaired a fault in it. So he got his drive and I got my curry.

One day I saw him and said that I thought that he looked tired. He said that he hadn't got to bed until really late the night before. He said that everyone was busy working, folding leaflets or some other task. He thought they were a dedicated, energetic bunch but hoped that soon they would finish for the night. There seemed to be no stopping them. He then said that he was tired and that he would have to go and get some sleep, and immediately everyone else started moving too. They had all been waiting for him to make the first move. He never realised how powerful they felt that he was.

On election day Jamie and I did the early-breakfast leaflet drop. My job was then to drive Jamie around all day to the different polling stations. This was great fun, except that by the middle of the afternoon we were both beginning to fall asleep due to late nights and the very early mornings. I learnt a lot about door knocking from this experience: where to stand, how long to talk for, and how to move on.

My job for the last week was to intervene after Jamie had been chatting for a while and then one of the London agents would take over from me. The agents would tell me when to intervene, but I was a quick learner and soon we had a slick team working.

Everyone wanted to go on the Battle Bus but people had to take it in turns. After a while Jamie insisted that I always went, as we made a good team, but I didn't get to the "count". He couldn't sway that one. There were far too many of the London gang there and so I had to wait back at base with everyone else.

As with many things in life, you can think in retrospect that it wasn't meant to be, and this was the case with Jamie winning the by-election. In fact, I've forgotten the name of the Labour man who won it, but the Conservative candidate won elsewhere in a later election. So I wasn't going to be the secretary to an MP.

A good bad experience

You may ask: how can you have a good bad experience? Well, I did.

I got a job working at an adventure playground in Birmingham. I won't name it as I don't know whether it exists any more and wouldn't want to upset the locals.

I worked with primary-aged children, but they were at school most of the time and so I was bored, bored, bored. My co-worker was okay but members of the management committee were a strange bunch who spent a lot of time flirting with each other. I was glad when I knew I was leaving but at about the same time my co-worker started confiding in me about his suspicion that money was being taken out of the organisation fraudulently. We went and consulted with a local worker, who didn't believe us. Cutting a long story short, when I left the police called me back to Birmingham to give a statement.

I suppose I learnt not to have faith in everyone.

A forgotten letter

One day I received a letter in the post inviting me for an interview for a job I had forgotten about. The interview was to take place in Beaconsfield, Buckinghamshire. I really didn't know where Beaconsfield was – as far as I was concerned, it was London. The job was to be a community worker in a village called Colnbrook. I looked on the map and found that Colnbrook was near Heathrow airport.

I rang up to accept the interview and decided that I would get the train, visit Colnbrook to have a look around and then get the bus to Beaconsfield for the interview. The interview was on 20th March 1983.

Being a city girl, I was used to having decent buses. We used to moan in Birmingham if we had to wait ten minutes for a bus and so, although I knew in principle about country buses, I didn't realise how bad they actually were.

I caught the train and after changes arrived at Slough. I then got the bus to Colnbrook, got off and walked around. I didn't know exactly what I was looking for but felt that the village, although very noisy from overflying aeroplanes, had a nice feel to it. It just seemed right being there.

And it was – I got the job and prepared to start work on 1st June 1983.

Chapter 7 – Colnbrook

I worked as a community worker in Colnbrook between 1st June 1983 and 31st March 1986, and it was one of the best working experiences I had had.

As I write this my closest friends from Colnbrook are coming to Gnosall for Matthew's day. Both my mum and I were thrilled that they were coming and it brought back so many memories.

I had at last achieved what I wanted to do. To be a community worker and work alongside local people, getting them to identify the issues that mattered to them.

I was employed by Buckinghamshire Social Services to work in a village that was just three miles from Heathrow airport. Tim stayed in Birmingham and followed me down to a computer job at Honda a year later. I went back to Birmingham most weekends for a year.

The day I got the job I was over the moon. The night before I started, I drove down and found the council flat which I was to rent before Tim and I bought a house in Bourne End. I had never driven so far and went for the first time on my own both on motorways and in a pub, both of which I did nervously.

Whether it was a good or bad omen I don't know, but the night I stayed at the flat there was an enormous, electrical thunderstorm and as well as being both excited and nervous about the next day, I was kept awake by the lightning and the rain lashing on the windows.

In later years, in our house in Bourne End, Tim and I would stay up watching the storms or I would snuggle down in bed and listen to the storm outside in the safety and warmth of my bed.

One Christmas Day many years before, in Birmingham, I had seen what looked like a very handsome distinguished-looking tramp walking the streets on a very cold Christmas morning. I often think of him and wonder whether he ever found anywhere warm to sleep.

A few days after I was in the flat I met my neighbour downstairs. He was a man in his mid-fifties and was retired due to a work accident. He told me that I was the first person he had spoken to since Christmas, other than when he was shopping, and I felt sorry for him. Unfortunately, he became a bit of a pest and so I was glad when Tim moved in and we eventually moved to Bourne End.

I had never worked for Social Services before and so wasn't sure what to expect. I had an office in Colnbrook but I rarely stayed in it as it wasn't the most inviting of places and was freezing cold. I soon acquired a Calor gas heater and became a strong woman, lifting refill bottles through a downstairs hall, up the stairs and through another room to my office – frequently I would knock the cylinders against my legs and Tim would remark on the increase in bruises on them.

On my first day I met my team leader at the Beaconsfield office, Helen, who became a friend. We had an intro chat and then I followed her to Colnbrook. We had lunch in one of the Colnbrook pubs and then she wished me luck. I was a fully fledged community worker and the Colnbrook community was in my hands.

My job description was to work with the local community. I knew the theory and now I had to see how it worked in practice. I thought that the first pitfall was my accent. Having a strong Brummie accent can at times be a disadvantage, but then if you have a university family background you can in fact have the ingredients to suit all kinds of people. I found that in Colnbrook there were people with all sorts of accents.

The village had become labelled as a problem, but its major fault was not in its people but in its political boundaries. When I started in Colnbrook it was divided into seven authorities: three counties, three districts and one parish council, which covered a third of the village. By the time I left we had had a poll using council ballot boxes and the locals had voted to join Slough, which the village subsequently did.

On this hot sunny day in June 1983 I walked around the village and then with a map found my way back to Burnham where I was living. I found out about and went along to the local groups, attended existing local meetings, helped at the struggling youth club and began to meet defined "significant local people". I was also contacted by the press and started what was to be a good working relationship with the local reporters and a long-term interest of mine.

I also met the other team members – a variety of characters, some of whom were very supportive to the idea of having a community worker, and others who had no understanding of what community work was about. They thought that it was an easy option but later admitted that they hadn't a clue about where to start.

Social work is about dealing with semi-defined problems of individuals, whereas community work is looking at themes which run through groups. It was my job to find what the real problems were in Colnbrook and to try to find resolutions if at all possible.

In those days I kept a diary of what I did and felt, which has been interesting reading since.

Door knocking

I decided to go door knocking. I knew that in theory there were two ways of doing this: either cold knocking, which meant just going and introducing myself, as I did with the Northfield by-election, or planned knocking.

I prepared a letter which I delivered to a number of houses a few days before I planned to visit. This was an effective way of working and I got to know lots of people, some of whom already belonged to groups and others who were interested in helping.

One day I visited a house and was bitten on the ankle by a little snappy dog. It really hurt and I remember swearing while I was on someone's doorstep. I cried all the way home and immediately rang Tim, who came home and took me for a jab up at the local A&E. The next day I went back to the couple that I had visited and apologised to them. They thought it was quite amusing and liked my natural human approach.

I had worked in a youth club many years before in Birmingham and for several weeks the kids had been an awful pain, trying to rule the roost. Well, one night I had had enough and I just swore at them. They were so shocked that I didn't hear a word from them all night, and they had a lot more respect for me from then on. I only did it once and it worked. But having a dog make you swear is just too much.

The whole time that I did door knocking in Colnbrook, no one ever swore at me or even shoved their door in my face. The majority of people were very keen to have a chat.

I'm not God

The trouble with door knocking is that you can endlessly go on doing it but then have nothing except a lot of responses to show for it. At some point you have to say, That's enough – I'll have to look at this lot and see if it makes any sense.

One of the problems that I had was that people would say, "And what are you going to do for us?" I've forgotten the number of times I said "I'm not God" in a humorous, jokey way. I made them aware of inaction – for example, Heathrow was trying to build another runway, which would have meant that a sewerage works would have moved closer to Colnbrook.

Colnbrook News

After I was door knocking for only a relatively short time I realised that the dominant theme which was emerging was that local people just didn't know what was going on. I decided to start a monthly newsletter. I wrote it, typed it, printed it and delivered it to sixteen hundred households. After about the third or fourth copy, with the help of a student I had on placement with me, we had a team of people to do all the work.

Colnbrook News continued after I left and was the means for the local community to express their concerns and unite.

What I wanted to write about in this book was the people who influenced me and how my life progressed. Colnbrook was like Victoria School, a place where I was very happy, but after a while I realised that I had reached, or was heading towards, the point that workers only dream of – doing themselves out of a job.

The local people in Colnbrook worked as a cohesive group even though there were times when I found myself acting as referee between two angry people. I was successful in Colnbrook, people responded to my ideas and developed them further themselves.

Apple Fayre

Phoebe, my daughter, still dresses up in clothes that I made for the first Apple Fayre in Colnbrook. During my research into the history of the village I found out that Mr Cox had developed his world famous Cox's Orange Pippin in Colnbrook. I, in my eccentric, loony way, thought that this was dead exciting and dreamed of apple-everything. Apple Fayre caught on and celebrations continued for a number of years.

Someone in Colnbrook was so excited that they sent a letter to the Mayor in New York from the Little Apple to the Big Apple and got a good luck wish back. My mum has memories of chopping and frying onions for hours on end, to put in burgers and hot dogs. We had huge queues of people waiting.

My friend Alan reminded me the other day of when Luke was pulled onto the stage during the revue, to audition for the part of the hero in a version of an old silent movie. Luke has always been a good mimic and so he decided to play the part with a strong Jasper Carrott accent. The audience cheered and Luke got the part.

There were people in Colnbrook who were special to me and had I moved to live there I might still be there now.

A chance

While I was in Colnbrook I worked closely with the local press. I would regularly get to meet reporters at public meetings and would contact them about things that were happening in the village. On one occasion I looked out of my office window and saw a horrendous snarl-up in the high street. Traffic had become a political issue in the village and so I rang the reporter I knew and told him to get there quick for a good story. He came on a motorbike with a photographer and got a good story.

From then on, if I wanted to get something in the paper, I did. Reporters would also bring me their draft articles concerning Social Services stories and ask me to read them before they were published. I often found that edited versions were published, which reflected my comments.

One of the local editors offered me a week's training, going alongside his reporters to see how the paper was put together. I told my boss about this offer but Social Services wouldn't let me do it. I wish I had taken a week's leave and done it for my own benefit, but that is looking from an older and more confident perspective.

False claims

My relationship with the press came into its own when a local Conservative candidate made claims that he had been instrumental in getting a pharmacist to open a chemist shop in Colnbrook. I was incensed because I had started the campaign through *Colnbrook News* and had never heard of this man. I contacted the editor, who, the following week, wrote an apology in the paper and gave the accurate information. I never did meet the candidate.

A wedding

I was so attached to Colnbrook that it seemed to be the right place for Tim and I to marry. So, on 25th July 1987, we got married in the church in Colnbrook. The vicar, Jeff, had become a friend, through my work in the village. I had spent many frustrated hours at the vicarage printing *Colnbrook News.*

One of the older women in the village had come with me, at 5.00am a couple of days before the wedding, to the international market to pick flowers. She decorated the church and the old village hall that we used for the reception. As a joke we had white and red table cloths that we laid in such a way as to look like the Red Arrows. It was a great wedding, with all the friends, old and new, who I wanted to be there.

Chapter 8 – Doing Social Work

Most of the purpose of writing this book is because social work gets so little day-to-day coverage in the media and so, although the first seven chapters are of great importance to me and made me the social worker I am today, it is the following chapters which tell in detail the tales of, in some cases, most traumatic lives.

As the media condemned Ian Huntley and Maxine Carr before they even stood trial in relation to the deaths of Jessica Chapman and Holly Wells, they knew little of why Huntley had already been detained in Rampton secure hospital under the Mental Health Act at the time of his being charged with the girls' murder. What social workers know, however, is that there are an awful lot of people who are damaged by events in their childhood who never have the opportunity to really understand what happened to them and why.

Social work should be about supporting people but is dominated by all kinds of procedures and criteria, many of which are linked to financial constraints. However, even with these constraints, the dominant theme running through social work is communication and building relationships.

When I left Colnbrook I worked as a community worker across the whole of the south Buckinghamshire area, but I was never as successful at motivating people. It was too large a geographical area with too disparate a population.

Buckinghamshire Social Services, as often is the case, had a reorganisation and there seemed no future in community work and so I thought I would have a go at doing social work. I talked to my boss about this but she wasn't very keen and said that although I had been an excellent community worker she wasn't sure what I would be like as a social worker.

I had been promoted through a formal progression through levels one (newly qualified) and two to three (very competent worker). I was told by Buckinghamshire personnel that I could take up a social work post but that I would have to take a drop in salary to level two. This was a kick in the teeth as I had known social workers who had become community workers and who had not had a decrease in salary.

I have found in my working career that there is a hierarchy, and a belief that some kinds of social care work are easier than others. This also means that unqualified people are employed. There is also a differential between working with adults and with children. For many years working with children was seen as more difficult, but in fact, having worked in both disciplines, there are skills developed in each which complement each other.

There have been an awful lot of changes since 1988 when I started doing social work. After feeling rather miffed about the money and status, I decided to look at social work jobs in neighbouring authorities. I rang up Slough, which at that time was in Berkshire, and asked about social work posts. They had two posts going, one in the long-term children and families team, the other in the intake team. I made an informal visit after applying for both. I started working as a social worker in August 1988.

Intake

When I started in intake I had to get used to the fast pace. It was like when I went from the nursery to West Heath hospital but in reverse.

I soon tuned into the new pace. At that time we worked with all kinds of clients, older people, children and families, disabled people and people with mental health problems. We were what they called the first point of call and had people ringing up and visiting the office. We were an extremely busy team, dealing with, in some cases, very stressful dramatic cases.

We did, however, also have our in-house perks – whenever there was a conference or training session running in our office, we got the leftovers. One thing that you don't know about me yet is that I love food. Being in a town with a high number of Asian residents meant that we had some really lovely nibbles, such as samosas. If there weren't nibbles there were biscuits or someone would go up to the chippy.

For food lovers we were the best team to be in, unless we had a team effort to slim. If people were slim when they started they either didn't stay long or they conformed to the norms of the team. Of course, there was the occasional person who seemed to keep that great figure, but they were few and far between.

Intake was an excellent place for me to start my social work. The team was, in some ways, a little gushing and huggy but besides that the standards were high. We gave people a good service, supported each other and produced good, clear, accurate documentation.

I loved working with the variety of people, not just the clients but the professionals too. Yet again, I learnt so much. Even little things can make an awful lot of difference to people's lives. For example, I learnt that if an older person was going for a short stay or to live in a residential home then the staff knowing how they like their tea or whether they have sugar can make the difference between feeling at home or feeling like a stranger.

The large throughput of people meant that you had to have your head in gear. However, when you met someone in Woolworths six months later who was updating you on the next six events of their life, sometimes – or, should I say, regularly – you had to play the bluff game so that they didn't know that you couldn't remember who they were. Suddenly it would come to you in the middle of a team meeting. I use the term "you" instead of "me" because it happened to all of us.

Much more dangerous though was playing the bluff game with a client who had come to the office at the request of the manager to discuss certain concerns about their parental role. If the manager was out and you couldn't find the file, it was a real bummer. How could you measure the short- and long-term risks? I usually managed to bluff okay. I only remember once underestimating risks, but it wasn't a life and death situation.

One of the things I have been able to do in my working career is to predict certain changes within political climates. I knew that community work had no future, as I knew that the intake team would specialise with children and families. To most of the team this change was fine as most of them preferred to work with this client group, but for two of us it was a disappointment. I liked the variety and my colleague preferred working with older people. But the inevitable happened, although not until just after I returned after Zoe died.

I was thirty-two years old when I started in the intake team. I had been ready to start having kids when I was about twenty-seven but Tim wasn't ready until he was thirty. When you really love someone you compromise in life, and so I waited.

We married when I was thirty-one and then Tim said he didn't want to try straight away because he thought that it would look like a shotgun wedding. When I think of it now the idea is quite amusing, having been together for fourteen years. So we waited.

We went on holiday to the USA and Canada a month after I started in the intake team and I conceived on the first attempt. Initially it was a little embarrassing as I hadn't been in the job very long. I didn't really want people to know until I got past the twelve weeks stage, but some had guessed earlier by the amount of pies and chips I had been eating – even for a food lover like me it was a little extreme.

While I was in Slough there were an increasing amount of referrals of teenage pregnancies and cases of sexual abuse. We also discussed evidence that indicated forms of ritual abuse.

Young social workers have often been accused of not knowing because they are not mothers or fathers themselves, and to a certain extent as a mother now myself this can be true, but then how we deal with our own children is different.

We saw some real nasty abuse and we had to deal with it and cope with it knowing that there was only so much we could do to protect the children we were working with. We weren't living with them twenty-four hours a day and with caseloads knocking thirty-plus and two days a week of duty, even the most organised of us couldn't see everything.

I fortunately (crossed fingers) have never personally been involved with a case of a child death by abuse and have great sympathy for professionals who have. I can also get very angry with the media when they condemn through whatever reason, whether it is ignorance, sensationalism or other unknown reasons.

They need to examine the constraints and increasing bureaucratic nonsense before they condemn. But the sad thing is that they could be helping, they could have real social workers giving their viewers and readers tips on what to do if they are stressed or see others in such a position.

My experience is that there are very few intentionally evil people in this world. The majority of cases of abuse or neglect are through different circumstances and general pressures in life.

Being pregnant heightened these feelings of the injustice towards children, but in many of the cases we worked with we could only measure risk by our own feelings or other people's experiences.

The current practice in social work is to try to use theory to what they call "inform practice". This means that you try to see patterns so that you don't repeat the cycle. Or perhaps you use formulas –

in other words, if you get seven out of ten of these certain factors, the chances are that you have a child at risk of a defined form of abuse. The difficulty in working in this way instead of with your gut feeling is that you do not take full account of the individual elements which create that unique scenario.

So if you think about that and all the information I have given you so far about myself, how would you measure me up? This is what social workers have to do every day and in lots of ways it's amazing how many times they do get it right. I'm not going to quote statistics because that doesn't suit this autobiography, but social workers throughout the UK work with an awful lot of people every day.

Being a pregnant social worker

Being pregnant is knackering at the best of times but when you've had a hard day at work which has included taking your fourteen-year-old young man to the latest childcare establishment for the third time in a fortnight, you do tend to crash out when you get home.

I really liked this kid. He was bright, a dropped-out grammar school kid who had been heartbroken when his mum and dad split up when he was ten years old. His parents continued not to get on very well and consequently he didn't see much of his dad. He developed a taste for nicking cars. They were always Fords, as he could get into them and start them easily. Initially he had just gone along with some other kids and had been a passenger but he soon started to drive himself. I told him that one day he might kill himself and that was probably the only way that he would get his head into gear.

I spent a lot of time taking him places, going to court with him, etc. Anyone who works in this field will know the ridiculous way that the court system works, with cases being adjourned time after time so that the young person comes to regard it as a joke. My youth wasn't as cocky as some. Underneath it all he was a decent bloke and it still happens today over a decade later.

I remember the first time I took him to what they called an "out of county placement". We set off for a place in Oxfordshire and on the way he had *The Sun* newspaper to read. I noticed that as he read he was sniffing. I didn't give him away until now because at fourteen it wasn't cool to cry.

One day I couldn't take him and instead a colleague went to the police station to collect him. He decided to do a runner. The worker came back to the office a little embarrassed. The next time I saw him I went mad at him, giving him a real telling off. I asked him what he thought the other social worker had felt, and he apologised and never did it again. He acted like a real gentleman. He would wait for me at the police station, reading anything he could about his rights. He became very good at the law. We would then manoeuvre ourselves out of the car park. He would often guide me so that I avoided bumping badly parked police cars. We would then set off to the next childcare venue, with him in charge of the map. We would chat on the way about life and the universe. We would arrive, I would stay for a short time and then start the homeward journey. The next day I would go to work to find that he had absconded and was missing (he was usually at a mate's house). This happened on numerous occasions. Sometimes he would stay for a while, but usually he would head back home and his mum would have him for a bit until he played her up again.

And this was only one case of many. In retrospect, a lot of this sounds ridiculous and it continues today because if someone is bloody-minded enough there is nothing you can do about it. The practical side of finding the accommodation each time was a nightmare, especially after he was a known regular absconder, but usually after several hours of frustration, rearranging all my appointments for the day or finding someone to cover my duty, I would manage to charm someone into having him.

Many of the young people I worked with were not as bright and pleasant as him; some you would think had come from another planet and keeping your cool with them was at times difficult, but they were all interesting. I suppose that one of the main reasons why I stay in this work is because most people really are very interesting.

One of the most fascinating cases I ever had was a thirteen-year-old girl called Cal. She was disabled with cerebral palsy and had been labelled as mentally handicapped, but she was far from it. She was as bright as a button. She lived with her mum, dad and brother and came from a semi-Westernised Asian Sikh family.

I learnt a lot from working with her and her family but one of the greatest lessons that I have passed on to the students that I work with is that you should always be careful of taking other professionals' advice when it comes to issues of culture.

Cal didn't want to go to the Sikh temple any more. It was her way of rebelling but her parents were finding it a little difficult because of what their relatives thought about her not going. I talked to an Asian colleague in the office, who gave me the name of one of the leaders of the temple. I had a chat with him about the possibility of Cal coming along to a girls' group held at the temple and said that I would have a chat with her family. I went to see them and they agreed to meet the rep from the temple and discuss the possibility of Cal attending.

It all seemed ideal, as I was concerned that Cal was getting rather isolated and needed some friends of her own age rather than just spending most her time with her family members. Well, I have never been so embarrassed in my life. The rep arrived and he immediately started shouting at the parents about the fact that they should force Cal to go to the temple. They sat quietly; Cal started shouting. I took her aside and he continued to shout at them for another twenty minutes.

When he left I said that I was so sorry for bringing him there. The parents said that they knew that he would do that and so I asked why they agreed to have him there. They said that they knew I was trying to help them and thought that at least I was trying.

I have never made that kind of mistake again – lots of others, but not that one.

Cal had a love/hate relationship with her mother. They couldn't live together without major incidents but they also couldn't live without each other. Cal spent two periods of time in care. On the first occasion she faked a catatonic state for several hours (the workers took advice, left her and six hours later she asked if she could go home). On the second occasion she screamed for several hours late at night, disturbing all the other children.

My first meeting with Cal was when she came to the office with her mum and she started lashing out at staff in the reception area. She wasn't going to talk to a male duty officer. I went out to see and managed to calm her down.

I worked intensively with Cal until I went on maternity leave. She was very angry about her disability. She had a sister who was still-born, who her mother had never finished grieving for. It was perhaps a sorry twist of fate that of all the social workers who Cal had assigned to her, it would be the one who lost her own baby daughter.

And I was just about to go on maternity leave when one day I came into the office. Everyone was looking at me in a strange way. They were a little scared of telling me. My young car thief had stolen a car, been chased up the M4 by the police and had ended up in intensive care.

A few days later a colleague went to visit him and he sent a message back to say he was sorry: I was right all along – he had nearly died and he had learnt his lesson the hard way. He had been given a second chance and he was going to get his act together. And apparently he did.

Chapter 9 – Zoe and Beyond

It's difficult and yet easy writing about Zoe. I know that this is a contradiction. But as Phoebe and Josh argue about something as mundane as which way to steer a pedal boat and Phoebe locks herself in the caravan toilet with her bag of make-up declaring that she will never re-emerge, it seems strange writing about Zoe.

When I was pregnant with Zoe I had one of those daft wedding rings things done over my tummy. You know, the ones which go round and round if it was to be a girl and swing back and forward if it was a boy. Yes, you are right: mine came out girl, girl, boy and that's exactly what I had. The only thing was that Tim and me planned to have only two children. Six months after Josh was born I was sterilised.

Zoe was a planned, wanted child. She was born in the early hours of 31st May 1989. After two days in hospital I came home and we started our new life as a family. We came back to the house that we had been renovating for many years (which is another part of my story).

I had forceps to help with her birth but that wasn't regarded as anything extraordinary. Zoe was very alert, taking in the world around her. I have pictures to show this alert young baby – and then at seven o'clock in the evening on 5th June she was dead.

We had decided to go to High Wycombe on the morning of 5th June, to register Zoe's birth. It was a nice sunny day and we registered her birth and then we found a nice little café for a drink. It was a perfect day, a day I had looked forward to for many years, and I was so happy.

We went back home and in the early evening I sat feeding Zoe. It was the first time that she had fed properly without either a breast shield or top-ups from bottles. When you have your first baby they fail to tell you how long it actually takes to get into a real rhythm of feeding. It's not surprising that so many people give up after a short time and have to cope with the sense of failure.

Well, Zoe fed and I felt happy. Tim was having a snooze in the bedroom, the room next door. I took Zoe through, put her in the cradle and turned to talk to Tim. I then looked at Zoe, who was turning blue. As Tim blew gently into her face I rang the labour ward, who told me to ring for an ambulance.

For years afterwards the sound of a 999 ambulance sent a sick feeling to my stomach. The ambulance seemed to take ages, but in fact it was very quick and we sped to the hospital. It felt as though we were going at about two hundred miles an hour and during the journey the ambulance man blew gently in Zoe's face.

The whole hospital building was, and remains, a blur to me. They took Zoe away and a nurse sat with us, trying to be encouraging. We just clung to each other. A doctor appeared at the door and gave a negative look to the nurse. We were then told that Zoe had died. They gave us Zoe and we cuddled her limp body and then gave her back to the nurse.

We were taken home by two policemen and sat silently in the car. One of the policemen continuously wiped his nose whilst the other openly cried. They stayed as short a time as possible.

That night was the longest and the most awful in my lifetime. We just clung to each other and cried and cried. We slept on our bed-settee as we couldn't face sleeping in our own bed without our little girl.

At the hospital they asked us who we wanted to tell and calls were made to both lots of our parents. They must have been the most awful calls to receive. My dad said, years later, that when the call came he initially thought that it was me who had died and that he felt relief that I was still alive, only then to feel guilt about his thoughts.

The next days and weeks were a blur. They say that time heals – well, I think that it steels you to things rather than heals. You begin to realise that there are not many worse things that can happen to you; at least that's what you think.

People said over the years how they feel that they wouldn't have coped, but it's one of those situations in life where you have only one of two alternatives – either you cope or you don't. Perhaps that's not quite true, as I believe that Tim never really got over Zoe's death, and number 26, our house in Bourne End, became a kind of mausoleum.

Zoe's death sent a ripple outwards – it didn't just affect us and our families. All the staff in the local surgery were distressed by her death. We had a wonderful GP who came to see us half an hour after we returned from the hospital and continued to visit us for some time afterwards. Years later, apparently, long after he had left the surgery he would ask how we were doing.

My boss, the other Tim, and supervisor came to see me at home and I planned to go back to work after I had had my six-week check. I would start by just working mornings and then, when I was ready, go to full days. I said that I wanted everyone to know about Zoe.

Getting up and ready for the first day back didn't seem as hard as I had thought. I arrived at work, walked into the office and within an hour was faced with three people who didn't know that Zoe had died. After about the sixth person my supervisor stormed into an important management meeting and angrily confronted them about the fact that so many people didn't know that Zoe had died. They said that they thought that it was for the best. She was livid.

After a week I went back to being full-time. Initially I was only working with older people but this didn't last for more than a few weeks. For months later I came across people who didn't know that Zoe had died, and often I had to put my arms around them and comfort them.

Remarkably, neither Tim nor I tried to lay blame on anyone for Zoe's death. We visited a paediatrician, Dr C, who was wonderful and obviously very good at his job. He asked us what we would like to know about the results of Zoe's autopsy. Did we want to know nothing, something or everything? We decided that we wanted to know everything. He said that there was no reason for her death and that as far as he was concerned as a human being she was perfect. He told us that she had working ovaries and lots of other detail which I cannot really remember. He also said that if ever we considered having another child that he would be pleased to work with us.

When I was three months pregnant with Phoebe I wrote to him and he wrote back return of post saying how excited he was. Tim and I had decided straight away that we wanted another baby and that we hoped that it would be another girl. It took seven months of trying to conceive Phoebe. In the meantime, I carried on working. Life carried on.

Getting pregnant again

I really don't know how people have the strength to carry on in their determination to have a child. Phoebe took seven months to conceive and I had visions of never being able to have another baby again. Zoe was in my mind every day and has stayed there on a regular basis ever since. She could never be replaced. She was unique. It is also interesting that I had said, before I was pregnant with Zoe, that if we had a little girl I would like to call her Isis after the Egyptian goddess of the moon.

As a child I had often thrown my bedroom window open when it was a full moon and talked openly to the moon. I have always felt better when it is a full moon. Edmund would say that the moon does have a significant effect on us. He says that Buddhists have done a lot of research into the effects of the moon, such as the increased incidence of accidents.

The moon to me is still very romantic and when Tim and I went to Egypt for our honeymoon the place I liked best was Philae Island, where Isis's temple is. So why Zoe didn't have her name I don't know: it was obviously meant for Phoebe, who has it as her middle name and whose first name is also the Greek goddess of the moon.

Eventually I got pregnant and Phoebe was due at the end of September 1990.

Routine

Life went on and a kind of routine started – that is, if you can call it that. I went to work, came home, snoozed, waited for Tim to arrive home at some unpredictable time, and worked on the house. Yes, there was a routine, but it certainly wasn't any that most people would recognise.

Number 26

At some point in my story I have to write, rather tortuously, about number 26 Somerset Road, Bourne End.

I don't know how it happened but when we started looking for a house we looked for something with "potential". Well, number 26 certainly had that. It was a bungalow built in 1929 with a reasonable amount of land around it and could – yes, could – have been a fantastic house. But what started as a wonderful dream became the ruination of Tim's and my relationship.

Anyhow, in 1989 we had owned number 26 for five years and at that stage we had no hot water or central heating and no roof on lots of the house. June, my mother-in-law, had rushed to paint the only two plastered rooms, one for a bedroom and one for a living room. It was, and continued to be, a nightmare, until on 2nd February 1997 I left it and Tim to go to live with Phoebe and Josh in Staffordshire. But until that day there is still a lot of story to tell.

More routine

After the few weeks of just working with older people I started yet again working with children. By now the management were making a move on splitting up our work. We would retain the short-term work with children and their families and the older people work would go to another team. So this kind of fitted in okay with my readiness to work with a lot of children again.

Suddenly we received a lot of referrals about children who were deemed to have been sexually abused. We had had some training on how to work with this, and in particular about non-leading questions, but mistakes were made as the tendency was to still go charging in like the cavalry to save the child from the evil hands of the abuser. We didn't go taking piles of children into care in the middle of the night, like in Orkney, but we also found it difficult to think logically rather than emotionally about the child. We learnt that children could be got at by their abusers and so we had to tread very carefully, balancing risk with the long-term best interests of the child.

As I see articles in the paper now or reports on radio or TV, I think if only we could tell you the truth. I have come to the conclusion, after being qualified for twenty years, that in lots of ways we can, but we have to tell the truth through the guise of the storyteller – the wise man or woman who sat in the market square and told of potential ills. I believe that we can, and this is the first attempt through opening up my life to tell some of these tales.

The youngest child that I worked with who was believed to have been sexually abused was eleven months old. Her abuser was believed to be her mother. It is often believed that most abusers are men, and that may be statistically true but the abuse that this woman was supposed to be undertaking was particularly evil. She was placing gadgets in her baby daughter's vagina. There was proof of interference but during the time I worked with her there was no proof – only a belief – that it was her.

I suppose that this case was even more heightened for me because of the loss of Zoe. Like a few cases I worked on at that time, I found myself handling her case robotically – that is, I hadn't really taken on board the emotional nature of the cases. We could not choose who we worked with. Social workers can't do that and most of us wouldn't want to anyway. Perhaps we are different – the fact that we believe that people should have more than one chance in life and that it isn't fair to throw someone around the circle of people, letting them fall on the way. They need to know that someone will keep a tight hold of them and say that now is the time to sort things – not tomorrow or next week, but now.

Of course, the sorting process is often time-consuming, and frustrating beyond belief. People and their circumstances really get to you. Sometimes it's impossible to shut them out, but at this time I was cruising on automatic pilot, until one day I went to a meeting at a foster carer's home. A colleague and I had taken a youngish child into care. My colleague was going out that evening and so the introduction of the child to the family was a little more rushed than I would have liked.

I went along to the planning meeting and criticism was made of the introduction. I just broke down in floods of tears – months of overdrive built up to that crescendo. Everyone understood, but I drove back twenty-five miles to the office in floods of tears and tried to creep into the office. My team were supportive and I did not continue with the case.

When I think back now, it is amazing how strong I really was. There were only a few occasions when I resorted to tears, but what happened was that I was prevented from doing things that I wanted to do and was good at. For example, my boss kept avoiding the discussion when I asked about having a student. I was doing much the same work as anyone else but I couldn't have a student. I began to think that I wasn't good enough at what I did but I found out from one of the training officers during a training session at Shirehall that my senior boss was trying to protect me from too much pressure because of Zoe. I was so cross because she didn't have the guts to tell me and I was really wondering about my own ability.

I have always tried to be straight and open with the people I worked with and was very flattered when I was in the position of supervisor to two members of staff a few years later and they both told me that they always knew exactly where they stood with me, as I had a skill of telling them when they had done things wrong in a nice, encouraging way.

The skills of social work

When I started social work I used to hide the fact that because my training had principally been in community and youth work I had had no casework experience on placement. I was fortunate to go to a good team who helped their staff develop good recording skills.

As a Practice Teacher now and for many years, I believe that, in fact, my assessment skills started when I was a young child and I started reading biographies and wondering why people did certain things at certain times and what things happened to change the circumstances in their lives. After my time with the psychologist during the school phobia phase, I began to understand people more and could see patterns in people's lives that were not dissimilar to my own. And so my knowledge and understanding of people has continued to develop and will continue throughout my life. What I feel is most important in being a social worker is an openness to new knowledge and an ability to compartmentalise that knowledge, not into fixed boxes but into multitudes of formulas and possibilities.

Whilst mathematics can be used to predict the probability of certain things happening in certain ways to certain people, what also has to be taken into account is that immeasurable percentage of the unknown. Social workers need to be able to follow the clear-flowing river and help push their clients through the dank swamps or quicksand back to that crisp clear-flowing water.

What I have found over the years is that I am increasingly using stories and metaphors to give meaning to what we do. For those of you who may be interested, take a look at some of my ideas in Part II.

A sad reminder and an angry social worker

I suppose because the public generally has little knowledge of social work and social workers, when passions rise about social workers' human failings, perhaps the public need to remember that we are just like anyone else. We have our strengths and we have our failings.

One of my own worst personal experiences was being "social worked" to by other social workers – basically I was bossed into something I didn't want to do while I was vulnerable.

When I was twenty weeks pregnant with Phoebe I went to visit the doctor for a regular check-up. He said that everything was fine, and I just burst into tears, saying it was fine last time too. He obviously didn't know what to say and asked if it would help me to have a scan. He immediately then said, "Well, I don't suppose you know whether it would or not." I said that I'd like a scan mainly because I liked them anyhow and thought that it was much more fun than watching TV.

I then stupidly decided to go to work. It was fine until someone came into the office who I hadn't seen for ages and who didn't know that Zoe had died. I comforted her and then found myself in an endless stream of tears.

My boss and a crowd of sympathetic social workers felt that the best thing for me to do was to go to a support group for parents who had lost a child from a sudden infant death. I agreed to go along a few days later to someone's house, at 7.30pm.

I had had a busy day and arrived to find only two other women who were both puffing like chimneys. One had had a sudden infant death and a miscarriage, the other had a small child and had lost another child. After about half an hour a health visitor came to join us. She grinned at us for the next two hours as these two women puffed away. I eventually made my escape and arrived home absolutely shattered.

I never went again. I had gained much more support from the older people I had worked with, who had in some cases shared their experiences of lost children, which they had longed to talk about and were able to relive through me.

One day I was on duty and I blew my top. As a worker I am generally regarded as laid back and was often brought in to deal with frisky clients. However, on this particular day we had an awful lot of referrals coming in together and had two child protection cases.

A regular client who was not allocated to a social worker came to the office asking for some financial help. We knew her well and were generally sympathetic to her situation, as she lived with two small kids in a drafty flat that she had difficulty heating. But on this particular day her manner was just too bolshy. One of the receptionists asked if I could talk to her as she was being a nuisance. I went through, apologised to her about the wait and took her into an interview room. She then shouted at me about her situation and how could I possibly know how she was feeling. As I said, I generally keep my cool but she continued in this line and she just hit a chord. I suppose I was terribly unprofessional, but I am a human not just a machine. I shouted back at her that actually she knew nothing about me and that at least she was fortunate to have two lovely kids, she hadn't lost a baby girl just a few weeks before like I had. She was totally shocked and apologised. She never caused a fuss in the office again. The next time I saw her I apologised but she said it was okay and knew that we always did what we could for her.

Games people play

One of the cases I had was of a woman who had three children, two young primary age and a young teenager. We had been asked to visit her by members of the Community Alcohol Team (CAT). She was a primary school teacher and had admitted previously to having a drinking problem.

I had been asked to do a spot visit. I suppose it was to see if we could catch her out. She wasn't in and I suppose it wasn't really the right thing to do but I had left a calling card. She rang the office and I arranged to meet her. When I arrived she admitted to having had a problem but said that she was okay now. She had had some counselling from CAT but after a couple of sessions had decided not to go any more. They had decided that she wasn't really ready to go it alone.

I went back to my boss and reported that I wasn't convinced by her and that perhaps I could visit again with the CAT worker. We fixed a visit and when we arrived she was in the kitchen knocking back the vodka in a very drunk state. The children were there and said that she had been drinking for hours. She poured out a tumbler of vodka while we were there and carried on knocking it back. After we had been there for half an hour a chap came in through the back door, swore at her and went away. According to the CAT worker, it was her estranged husband.

When we later went to court to get a supervision order they tried to deny that this had happened as he had not taken responsibility for his children. I had carefully recorded all that he said, including the swear words, which I wasn't sure how to spell. His solicitor suggested that co-operation would be more effective.

It isn't just clients who play games. Other professionals can be extremely good at passing the buck or not taking full responsibility.

Readers may be aware that each authority in the country has what is called a Child Protection Register. To be placed on the register a Child Protection Conference has to be called, which nowadays includes parents but in the 1980s generally didn't. Children can be registered under different categories but the category I always found the most difficult to get registered was emotional abuse.

I remember a fourteen-year-old Muslim girl who I had registered for severe emotional abuse, who, I found out through the grapevine, was being taken against her will to Pakistan. She had never even been to visit, let alone lived there.

I found out what flight she was on and went to the Chair of the Panel to ask if I could go and talk to her. He said that there was nothing we could do and that we should just let her go. I remember feeling very angry and sad for her. It seemed to make a mockery of the child protection system. I heard through the grapevine that she was taken to a small village and I never heard of her coming back again.

I hope that if any journalists read this book they will realise a lot of the sadness and tragedy that we have to work with, but along the way there is also warmth and feelings of comradeship. Social workers, on the whole, still have a belief that things can change for the better.

A new baby and a new job

Phoebe Isis was born on 28th September 1990, the day after my birthday. In fact, I spent the last part of my birthday in labour. I had spent the morning feeling fed up so Tim decided to work at home. I decided to go swimming but returned still fed up. At 6.00pm I announced to Tim that I wanted him to go shopping with me, so off I wobbled to Tesco. Around ten-ish I went to bed. Phoebe was born at 6.13am the next day. Tim went straight to the register office to record her birth. We were both over the moon having another girl.

After a week at High Wycombe hospital I went with Phoebe to Great Ormond Street Hospital for them to do some extra tests on her. My experience at High Wycombe was great, with the wonderful Dr C, but Great Ormond Street, well, it was such a dump.

I slept with Phoebe in what was like a cubicle, with very little privacy – even the cleaners would come in without knocking. I had to go down three floors to get to a toilet, which by 10.00am each day was overflowing with sanitary towels. I was going to eat in the hospital café until I heard, and it was confirmed, that there were several cases of food poisoning, so I went to a supermarket to get some food and had to leave Phoebe with the nursing staff.

Many of the children on the ward were pre-school age and yet there was nothing much for them to do. Parents had come from all over the country, some coming on a very regular basis. They told me of their stories and the many mix-ups in dates, etc. The nursing staff had little experience in play. I found myself several hours a day playing with some of the children, and gave the nurses some ideas of what to do.

It was an awful experience and Tim couldn't get to see us very often as it took three and a half hours each way to get there, with the traffic. I just couldn't wait to go home and when I was in hospital with Josh I pleaded with Dr C not to let me go there again. Fortunately I never had to. I just hope that it is a lot better today. I was so surprised by this place, which had such a good reputation, but none of the staff could compare to Dr C and his team.

I knew before I went on maternity leave that it would be pretty impossible going back to my job in the social work team, as the hours were so unpredictable. I relied totally on paid childcare as I did not have any family members living near me.

I often wonder why the obvious isn't told when they talk about a shortage in social workers. You cannot be in two places at the same time. When Stephen calls or texts to say he's off on one of his marathon journeys, taking a kid a hundred or so miles away, I know that I'll be lucky to see him before midnight. You just can't work that way when you have young kids and even if you had teenagers I imagine you wouldn't want to leave them that long.

One day I rang personnel about something to do with my maternity pay and asked them if there were any interesting jobs going. They told me that there was a job for thirty-two hours a week as a Respite Care Co-ordinator working with children and adults with learning disabilities (formerly known as mental handicap). The closing date was that day. They rang the manager and said that I was interested and asked whether he was willing to receive my application after the closing date. He said he was. I applied, got the job and negotiated to work my time over four days, starting from March 1991. I was to work there until August 1996.

Chapter 10 – Refining the Skills

The government had decided that social work must be divided into two distinct groups. These were the "purchasers", who would assess the needs of "service users" (clients), and the "providers", who would provide the service depending on the assessed needs. In 1991 the Children Act and the National Health Service and Community Care Act were both in their implementation stage and much was made about providing needs-led assessments. What this meant was that social workers should work with their service users to look in detail at their specific needs. What it meant in practice, sadly, was that it was a dream which would never reach fruition for many service users because the majority of social workers did not have enough imagination to fulfil this dream and because the increasing bureaucratic accountability was soaking up any additional funds or time that workers had.

My job was to recruit local people to act in a voluntary capacity to befriend adults and/or children with a learning disability. Much of the reasoning behind this was to give their families a break and enable able-bodied siblings to have some quality time with their parents on their own.

When I arrived the scheme had been running quite successfully for a few years. However, the recording systems relied very much on the memory of the worker. Over the next few years I, with two colleagues, developed good recording and communication systems where we could easily find out what was happening with each of our carers. Also, we not only increased the number of carers but also we had carers from more varied backgrounds, including several from Asian and Afro-Caribbean backgrounds.

The only problem that I had with the job was that, compared to working in intake, everything was so slow and I found that by the middle of the week I was getting bored.

The cause

As you can probably tell by now, I am someone who likes to take up a cause and if I believe strongly in that cause I will stick at it through thick and thin. Of course, my current cause is developing a better relationship between social work and the media, but in 1991 it was making sure that two excellent people were approved as respite carers.

Their names were Kevin and Alan. They were a gay couple and were very keen to become respite carers, and in fact were thinking of becoming full-time carers. They were very open with me about their sexuality and talked about the ways in which they had suffered discrimination.

When I assessed carers I used myself as a benchmark – in other words, would I be happy having this person look after my daughter and how would she get on with them? Kevin and Alan were warm and full of life and I knew that they would not only care well for anyone they looked after but also be fun to be with.

How did I know? Well, to answer this is the old debate: are social workers born with a special insight or do they just learn to judge on the balance of probabilities? Gut feeling has always been a little disputed but I think that my gut feelings have been accurate on so many occasions that there must be something in it.

I just knew that Kevin and Alan were right for the scheme. My boss was in full support of me and so I completed the assessment, wrote the report and took them to the Respite Panel. This didn't mean that I took them literally – just their report. Respite carers were told afterwards whether or not they were accepted.

The panel was rather incestuous, being made up of respite

workers and their managers from half of the districts within Berkshire, and some of the workers, although pretending to be open-minded, were rather conservative in their thinking. At times I was a terror with these panels because of some of the nonsense reasons they gave for why people shouldn't be approved and the criticisms which were made.

In later years I had one potential carer who had had a horrendous childhood with a stream of abusive stepdads but through this experience she was one of the warmest, most sensitive people I had known. The panel decided to postpone her approval and I told them that they would probably lose her as she would probably get a paid job in caring and that is exactly what she did.

It's interesting how, because of equal opportunities, anyone applying for a caring job doesn't have to share anything about their background or upbringing and yet we went into great detail about people's background and attitudes. I remember that we produced a questionnaire for potential carers to complete prior to the assessment process. We would help them with it if they preferred but it was a means of us being consistent with our questioning. The first question we had was concerning the carer's views of what constituted abuse. I remember some of the other respite carers being very critical of this but I believed that we were being open and to the point. We wanted two things for the people we worked with. First, that they be safe, and secondly, that they have a nice time. Anything else was just a bonus.

Anyhow, Kevin and Alan went to the panel and, as I predicted, they didn't get through. It sounds a bit like doing a driving test and I suppose in some ways that's exactly what it is like. Fortunately, the two reasons that were given could be rectified quickly and they were philosophical about not getting through first time. I took them to the next panel and they were approved, although some panel members commented that some parents may not want their children matched with them. A year later they were the most requested carers that we had.

Gut feeling

I have talked before about gut feeling. Nowadays I may be bordering on areas which are more controversial and perhaps thinking about psychic powers. There simply is no reasoning behind gut feelings – you just know that something is wrong.

I remember once when I was in the intake team reading a line on a very small file containing about eight words and I knew that there was something wrong with this family. I said to my boss that, instead of inviting the lone father to the office in response to his request for support, I wanted to do a home visit. This father was bringing up three children and was finding the middle child rather difficult. On file we only had a couple of letters. There had been no social work involvement.

I went to the house and sat in the living room. I chatted to the dad for a while as the child in question was out playing, although the dad wasn't quite sure where. Within a few minutes the child appeared and seemed happy to come and have a chat with me. We talked about how things were going and he said that he wasn't very good at doing what his dad said.

As a social worker you often want to survey the land. You can quickly look at a room or pick up sounds, looks, smells, etc., but I also liked to see what toys kids had to play with. Messy or untidy houses are not an issue to most social workers, unless there is evidence of dangers such as bare wires or paints with young children around. There was no evidence of any particular dangers in this house but there were no toys.

I assumed that the toys were up in the bedrooms and after quickly ascertaining that there were three bedrooms I asked the dad if I could take his son to let him show me his toys. Dad was happy with that and he was keen to show me and so the three of us went upstairs. When we reached his bedroom I had a shock – it reeked of urine and the carpet was completely sodden. I made no comment. The dad immediately apologised and said that he couldn't get him to go to the toilet; he would wee anywhere. Two of the walls also had great chunks taken out of the plaster. The father also pointed out to me that his son had tried to set fire to both the walls and the curtains.

This child appeared to be happy and well adjusted, although a little out-of-control. Dad then took me next door to the boy's sisters' bedroom. He told me that the younger of the sisters, who was six and the youngest of the three children, used to hide faeces in different parts of the toy cupboard.

I later asked the dad on his own why he hadn't asked for help before. He said that he had but no one had come back to him. He had asked the headteacher and she said that she would contact Social Services. I said that we had no record of her getting in touch.

I went back to the office a little overwhelmed. The next day the eldest child told a neighbour that she had been sexually abused by an uncle who had been living at the house. All the evidence in the bedrooms would have indicated long-term abuse.

As respite care workers we could potentially assess anyone in the community to be a carer. Sometimes we would find people who straight away we would think were not suitable because of their attitudes. We would not have, for example, anyone who was outwardly racist. If anything, we would normally give people the benefit of the doubt and start the assessment process to see if they were suitable or not.

However, on one occasion I had a young married woman who I went to visit. I got on fine with her but there was just something about her that I couldn't put my finger on. I came away having arranged to meet her again and went back to the office. I spoke with my boss and said that for some reason or other I felt that she suffered from Munchausen's Syndrome by Proxy. Now this is a very dangerous accusation because sufferers will tend to be very caring towards children, if not too much so, and then they secretly make a child ill. This young woman had worked in a residential unit for children with learning disabilities and she said that one of the community nurses in the office who visited the unit, who I knew well, had suggested that she become a respite carer.

For the next few weeks I visited her, undertaking the assessment, and became more and more suspicious. She seemed to have a fascination with the nurse Beverly Allitt, who is in Rampton Hospital for child murders.

What also didn't fit was the community nurse recommending her. This nurse and I often used each other to suss out views on particular areas of work. I hadn't seen much of her due to annual leave and other work commitments, but one day I caught up with her and after us both exchanging strange looks I suggested that we had a chat. She immediately asked me why I was assessing the young woman to be a carer. I said that I thought she had recommended her and I shared my suspicions with her. She then said that there was no way she would want her to be a carer and she filled me in on a number of strange incidents that had happened during her time working with the children.

We shared the information with my boss and I shared my concerns that she might try to volunteer somewhere else. In fact, I wasn't totally wrong as she applied to be a registered childminder. At the time she was pregnant herself and so we had an excuse for not approving her as we felt that she should see how she got on with her baby first.

It wasn't hard for us as we didn't have to approve anyone or give reasons for not approving them, but it became a bit of a nightmare for the under-fives workers as she had a right, if she fulfilled all the criteria, to be a childminder. I heard that soon after her baby was born she took it to the hospital one day, concerned about its health. I often wondered what happened to her.

This shows that systems are far from perfect. The under-fives workers would not necessarily have had any suspicions unless I had voiced them.

Baby two and two other things to do

I suppose I should say baby three because that's what it was like for Tim and me but you can't be morbid all your life and so when people asked how many kids we had, after a while we decided not to tell all and sundry about Zoe. She was always very much there but we didn't want to put the burden of her loss on new folk.

In 1992 I was getting a bit bored and so my boss encouraged me to do both my Practice Teacher's course and a Further Education Teacher's course. I had to do some teacher's practice and so ran a course on communication for students undertaking the BTec 1st in Caring.

Quite a few of the students could have come straight off an earlier caseload list. Several had suffered bullying at school or had had passing liaisons with social workers. Many of them aimed to get onto the nursery nursing course the next year but their academic level and motivation were questionable. It was hard work keeping them interested. I got through the course and was offered some paid work the following year.

The Practice Teacher's course was a formal way of working with social work students. When I did the course, the CQSW was still the formal qualification. I had my first Diploma in Social Work student the following year and have continued to have students ever since.

In the background of all this, and carrying the lump around which would be Josh, was number 26. I had decided that there wouldn't be enough room for us four in one room and so had moved us around the house. Tim's motivation to get stuff done was low and I suppose I did a cover-up job. And so I did courses and other things.

I had dreamed of staying at home with my second child and running a fantastic kids' club for professional parents. I would buy a minibus and take the children out to do exciting things. We would have a secret codebook where I would give each child individual messages. It would be my project run the way I wanted.

I had worked in so many places where the potential had not been fully explored and so that is what I wanted to do. But number 26 got in the way. It remained a nightmare wreck and is still that today. Hopefully by the time I have finished this book I won't own it any more and the nightmare will finally be finished.

Many weekends I would go and visit my parents, leaving Tim and his dad to get on with some work, only to return to an increased level of mess, which I would straight away have to tidy up. Sometimes I watch these DIY fix-it programmes on TV and wonder what the BBC would have made of number 26.

Joshua Ian

Josh was born on 23 August 1992 a remarkable day because I worked out that my last period before conceiving Zoe started on the same date in 1988 and so my child-bearing was completely contained within those four years. Josh was born at 5.15pm on a Sunday.

I had sworn that there was no way that I would have an epidural, and the junior doctor who saw me at the antenatal clinic told me to keep an open mind. When the time came I was so knackered that I succumbed – and guess what? Of course, the doctor was on duty. He was very good about it though and didn't make much fun of me.

I knew Josh was going to be a boy as I had had a test for Down Syndrome. Fortunately I did not have to make a decision and wonder now whether I could have had an abortion or not. I was so lucky that I didn't have to decide.

Josh isn't an easy kid; he's interesting but he's not easy. Sometimes he just goes on and on and on and I get mad with him and so my level of understanding of how parents can lash out has increased. At other times he can be the most charming of children, and fortunately that is his public persona.

Redundancy and a new way of life

On my birthday in 1993 Tim was made redundant. Mum and Dad had come by train to visit me. I walked down to the station with the children to meet them and as we walked up the road, there was Tim driving past. He put a good face on it but he was deeply upset and panicky. He had received a lump sum of redundancy money, which soon got soaked up in the building project. He spent hours woefully talking about never getting any work again, but in fact within a very short time he was headhunted. There were two possible jobs immediately on offer. One was a manager's post, which would mean that we would have to move to near Basingstoke, and the other was a consultancy, which would entail some travelling with the job. Of course, I favoured the manager's post, but I knew that Tim would be bored with it and so kept my mouth shut. He, of course, went for the consultancy and the travelling meant that he was away most weeks, leaving on the Monday morning with a family wave-off and arriving home on the Friday night.

I suppose in lots of family circumstances this would be a bit lonely but not too much of a problem, but I felt like the single parent and to top this I had to deal with number 26, living in a wreck.

For much of this time Tim and I were living in one room while the children had our bedroom as their room. We slept in the kitchen-cum-bedroom-cum-living-room on two settees. During the week I slept on one settee and the other had racks of washing drying on it. When I look back now, I wonder how I did any of it. Just getting enough dry clean clothes for us was a tremendous effort. Sometimes I went to the launderette, but with two young children it was such a drag.

I also used to keep everything in that room so that I only had one room to heat. When the children went to bed I would get into bed and watch the TV. I put an electric radiator in their room to take off the chills. Phoebe says that she remembers her bedroom being freezing cold. When I told them bedtime stories, I would get under the duvet with one of them to keep warm. The other would usually crawl in as well.

Immediately after Tim was made redundant I applied for another part-time job working for Buckinghamshire Social Services for a temporary period as a Practice Learning Co-ordinator. This entailed me arranging placements for social work students, supporting other Practice Teachers and supervising some of the students myself. One of the students, Clare, I have stayed friends with ever since and she recently came to stay with us; we hadn't seen each other for about six years.

And so for a period of seven months I did my usual job as a respite care worker, taught once a week and worked as a Practice Learning Co-ordinator. Each night we returned to a cold, overcrammed house. After seven months I was asked if I would like to stay on, on a month-by-month basis (as the funding was uncertain), but as I had applied and been accepted on an MA course, I declined.

In 1994 I started an MA in Public and Social Administration at Brunel University.

My day each week

I went to Brunel University one day a week for two years and I loved it. The feeling of doing something just for me and no one else. Of course, it wasn't just one day a week as I had to do the assignments and yet again I wonder how I did it, given the conditions I lived in and all the other pressures. During that time Tim only took the children out for one day to give me a chance to do my assignments, which showed his self-centred streak. Stephen is very different – he has told me to go off to the caravan to write and maybe some day I will but when you've always had to be around it's hard to change.

So I loved my one day a week, but I had to pay for childcare for Phoebe and Josh. This meant that over half of what I earned went on childcare. The course was interesting in its way but I was keen to do some European study options and both were dropped. This was rather disappointing.

The most interesting course that I studied was run by the Dean of the faculty. He had been a civil servant and had then become an Open University lecturer before he became a professor at Brunel. He was a bright, thinking, challenging man who loved lively debate. I really enjoyed his sessions and consequently got the best mark for his assignment.

I have never been a great marks person and I envy Phoebe who, even at eleven, achieves good results. She did a cornet exam last year and she never practices but she got a distinction, and recently she did a singing and drama exam and got honours. I reckon that the best exam I ever did was the eleven-plus. I still dream of the day when I will get a distinction for something.

Well, I had two years of my own day each week and then I started to prepare for my dissertation. This was a problem because I was doing the course for me and so wanted to do something I was really interested in, but my tutor kept rejecting my ideas. What I wanted to do was to look at how communication was taught to social work students. I was very concerned that there was an assumption that students knew how to communicate and I believed strongly that the complex nature of communication wasn't being explored fully. If you want to read more about this, look at communication awareness in Part II.

During this period my school phobic feelings showed their ugly head again and I began to feel that I was no good. I had achieved a fifty-five per cent overall mark, which wasn't brilliant but was enough to do the dissertation and, given my life circumstances, was pretty good really, but I began to feel hopeless.

No future

By 1996 I began to feel that I had no future. I had had enough of the respite care and decided to do sessional work lecturing. I managed to get the equivalent of half-time teaching social studies to nursery nurse students.

Tim was still working away a lot and the house was getting to me. It was an embarrassment. There were very few people who I would invite there and so I was very lonely. Each time I went with the children to visit my parents I came back and immediately walked into this cold dreary house to a dreary life with no future.

I have always been a dreamer but I found it hard to dream of anything because there didn't seem to be any point.

Tim came home stressed out. I never mentioned the house. I just lived in it. Every Saturday morning I had a grumpy Tim. I soon learnt to go out to shop with the children to avoid Tim until the afternoon when he would liven up. I understood why he was like that, but in lots of ways that just made it worse.

I had made a friend of a mother from Phoebe's nursery and spent some nice peaceful stimulating times round at her house. One of my friends was going through a rough patch too and so I saw very little of her. Tim's dad, Bob, still came to stay a lot on the pretext of doing the house, but although I was quite happy for him to come, his eating habits were very conservative and so it was much more effort making meals.

Changes in the air

I suppose it was inevitable that things wouldn't remain as they were. I was supposed to do more with my life and to save the children from this dreary life.

It is often relatively little things that can cause change. Tim had a colleague at work who owned a house which he rented out, near to Disneyland in Florida, and so we fixed to go there and then have a cruise of the Caribbean afterwards. This was to be our dream holiday. Tim told me later that he thought it would also give us proper time to talk about our lives generally.

Well, it was all booked except for the flights there and back. It was going to cost a fortune (the kind of money that Stephen would never anticipate). I started ringing for flights in the July (we were due to go in the following March). I could get flights there easily but I couldn't get us back.

It was absolutely driving me up the wall. I was so frustrated and stressed by it. It began to cause all sorts of arguments and I began not to eat. This was fine as I was overweight anyhow, but when I carried on losing weight and started having bruises all over me just from carrying things (Tim was never violent), Tim insisted that I went to the doctor, who did a thyroid test but found there was nothing wrong with me.

Once I invited my new friend and her husband and children around for a meal, which took an awful lot of pre-planning to get a decent space to put a table and chairs. I produced a decent Sunday lunch and then found that I couldn't eat any of it.

So I wasn't eating and Tim didn't really notice.

Anyhow, what really caused the change was Christmas. Tim invited his mum and dad to stay without thinking where we would actually put them. We eventually worked out what we would do after Tim said that there was no point doing any more building work.

They came and Christmas wasn't as bad as I thought it would be. After the actual festivities they said that they would stay on to help with the house a bit. Well, one day June and I started putting all of the tools together and when Tim saw what we had done he moaned that he would never be able to find anything. I said I'd put it all back as he wanted.

Tim's parents went home and life, if you could call it that (it was more of an existence), carried on. I eventually got the flights sorted out for the holiday but by then I had no interest in the holiday at all.

Chapter 11 – No Regrets

On 2nd February 1997 I decided to take the children swimming and had rung my new friend to see if she would like to join us with her kids. We had been a few times together and it had been fun, as we could have a nice chat about life and the universe. My new friend was very different from me. She worked for Glaxo as a scientist and both she and her husband had PhDs.

Anyhow, we were in the pool and I suddenly found myself bursting into tears. The pressure had become too much. After swimming we went back to her house and I decided that I was going to go and stay with Mum and Dad. I rang Mum and asked if it would be all right to stay.

I went back to number 26 with my friend and left the children at her house. We filled up two black bags with clothes. I remember just shoving them in anyhow and not really knowing what I had got. I went in the living room where Tim was sitting doing some work on his laptop and said that I was going to Mum's house. He continued sitting there and I left the house, went back to my friend's house and took the children and drove to Staffordshire.

I remember that drive as vividly as the ambulance journey with Zoe. I cried the whole way. I arrived and spent much of the next week crying. Tim rang up but for about a week I couldn't talk to him.

It is interesting that even when you are distressed to this extent that you can suddenly have bursts of inner strength as if you have a guardian angel watching over you. I was brought up as an atheist and sceptic and would still not believe in the Christian definition of God but I do feel that there is something beyond current human understanding.

Anyhow, I was on my way to Gnosall, to a new life of the unknown, and I have never regretted that move for one day.

The holiday

One of the first problems I had was that we had the famous holiday booked for seven weeks later. I said that I didn't want to go, but I did eventually go.

Yet again, I think now, how did I actually go? And how did I actually enjoy it quite a lot of the time? I suppose when your life is turned upside down, it all changes and it becomes difficult to know what is the norm.

We went to Disneyland, did the parades, swam in the pool at the house, drank, ate meals, and lived what, from an outsider's point of view, was a kind of normal life. We didn't argue because there wasn't anything to argue about. Tim tried to talk about things but what could we really talk about? It was obvious that there would not be any remarkable changes. He still wanted to do the same job, which meant that he would still have limited time to do the house, and there wasn't anyone who he trusted to do the house the way he wanted.

We went on the cruise and that was quite nice too, but if you are not a formal kind of person, well, don't go on one of these cruises as there is a strict dress code and hours of waiting for meals.

We arrived back at Heathrow and Tim helped us take our bags to our bus that would take us to Reading station, where we got the train back to Stafford. He never looked back. I expect he was too sad.

That woman

Tim and I had not only been a couple, but we had been best friends, but the last few years had emphasised the couple role, and best friends took second place. After moving to Gnosall, I would ring Tim about the children but often we would ring each other just for a chat. There were phases when I wouldn't hear from him for a bit and only the children would speak to him, and then there were times when he would ring for a chat, knowing that they were not around.

It was strange because he would talk to me, as a best friend, about me as "that woman". It was as if he saw me as two distinct women. The one who left with his children and the best friend.

Some regrets

My major regret was that Tim so stubbornly stayed at number 26. He could have been happy if he moved but he was too stubborn.

I always hoped that he would find a new woman in his life to be happy with. His work seemed to take over his life. He saw Phoebe and Josh but not as much as I would have liked. I was determined for the first three years to keep their relationship with him going and then I began to leave it more up to the three of them. I would drive the children over a hundred miles to pass them over to Tim and then drive back home to a quiet but cosy house.

Four moves in two years

We lived with Mum and Dad for six months. One weekend we were meeting Tim at Stratford-upon-Avon, where his parents lived, and I was thinking that I should start looking for somewhere to live. The problem was that I didn't have a job and Tim was giving me money for the children and so, although I was claiming unemployment benefit, I didn't want to claim income support as it would just get too complicated.

When I arrived back Mum had had the same thoughts and had seen a two-bedroomed house for rent at the other end of the village. Dad had rung up to find out its availability and I went to have a look. When I arrived the man who owned it said that another person was supposed to have come but hadn't turned up. So without any effort I got somewhere to live. Dad paid the rent, which I felt guilty about, but at the time he said that maybe one day I could help them out. Strangely, I am now doing this, as Mum is buying a house off me which I continue to pay the mortgage on.

This was a great little house and we had a very happy year living there.

After getting a job I went to my bank asking about mortgages and was told I could have £40,000. I started looking for houses. Tim said that he could top this up. I asked at all the estate agents. I wanted us each to have a bedroom. Phoebe was now seven and Josh was five.

One day an estate agent asked if we would consider a bungalow. I initially said that I wasn't keen but there were so few properties in Gnosall and the children were keen to stay because they were making lots of friends. I decided not to tell the children yet but would take Mum and Dad to have a look. I thought that they would be unlikely to like it as it was an old bungalow and it was on the main Newport Road.

We went to have a look and decided straight away that, even though it needed some work doing on it, it would be right for me and the children. It had a big garden and one neighbour was the Methodist church. This would later become a family joke about having God as our neighbour.

And it was warm – it had radiators that were not too old, it had been rewired and, with a bit of dampcourse and a lick of paint, could be lived in straight away. This was *The Dell*, and me, the children and loads of their friends would spend two very happy years here.

One of the best occasions at *The Dell* was Bonfire Night. We invited Phoebe and Josh's friends and their families. I provided the venue, bonfire and food, and everyone else brought the fireworks. We had stacks of them. It was also quite fun because the Boys Brigade held their bonfire night next door in the grounds of the Methodist church and so our kids got a double helping of fireworks.

Our Bonfire Nights seemed to define the traditional roles. The dads set off the fireworks, while the mums helped me with food. The kids just had a great time hanging out together. In fact, we used to have quite a few kids come and hang out. Josh was lucky to have a boy next door and one across the road to play with. Sometimes I would join in and invent a few wacky games, often based around dressing up.

We used to have musical dressing up, which meant each time the music stopped you had to go and put a piece of clothing on. It was usually Josh and boys that came back with the funniest outfits. One day Phoebe and her friend Sarah dressed up and asked about playing musical dressing up instead. I challenged them to dancing on the front lawn to the whole of ABBA's "Dancing Queen". The front lawn faced onto the road, which was the main road through the village, and so had a great deal of traffic passing by.

They took up the challenge and I rolled with laughter, tears running down my cheeks. It was so funny. They continued from "Dancing Queen" to a few more ABBA songs as the reaction of the passing traffic was just so hilarious. Most cars waved, a few grimaced. A motorcyclist gave them a very dramatic salute kind of wave.

These were the mad days, where I began to live again. We still met, and talked regularly with, Tim but we had another life too.

Sorting out work

It took me some time to get some work. I started applying in April 1997 and got a job as a Practice Teacher working for Staffordshire Social Services, which started in the November. This was an annual contract and had been such for about fifteen years. I worked half-time and I had a colleague who worked full-time. We had a number of students to supervise and also made links with the local universities, which provided the courses.

After the first year I began to realise that the chances of continued funding were limited. My prediction turned out to be accurate. My colleague went back to the job from which she had been seconded. My boss offered to keep me on until the end of December as she needed someone to arrange the placements as the usual worker was on maternity leave. This arrangement suited me as I could then work with students independently from the following January.

I had tried applying for some part-time social work jobs but seemed to get nowhere as I was told that I was not up to date. I had never been out of social work – I had just been a provider rather than a purchaser.

I found it extremely frustrating as every week I would hear about the shortage of social workers. I had also spent a lot of time trying to find a refresher course but there were none anywhere in the country.

Since 1997 I have worked as a Practice Teacher and in November 1999 I started to do agency social work. In 1999/2000 I worked as a social worker in a hospital team, working with older people. In 2000/2001 I worked until March in a children and families team and until July in a team for older people. In 2001/2002 I worked in another children and families team.

Bureaucracy gone mad

When I last worked with children and families we had good recording systems. What has happened recently is that the amount of paperwork and policies and procedures has just gone berserk. Whenever there is a child death and an inquiry, we hear that "lessons must be learnt". What are those lessons? Well, usually it's the next pile of procedures and new set of forms.

A Martian looking down on us could really have a good laugh at all this ridiculous nonsense because what it always fails to do is to realise that human beings are really just imperfect. We are not machines. Of course, like most social workers, I try to fill in what I'm supposed to fill in, but wonder who it is that creates all these new forms.

Some of the forms are for children who are in care – or, as they are nowadays called, "looked after" children. Well, that term in itself can lead to all sorts of views. Looked after? Well? Badly? In what way? Aren't my kids being looked after? This is certainly a great one to confuse a Martian. Why don't we just tell the truth? They are kids living with substitute parents.

Well, the forms that are used are just totally loony. This is my book and no one is going to stop me saying what I think. They were produced for people who have nothing better to do than spend all day with one child playing "let's do challenging quiz games". They are so daft. And they are starting to get the same over-the-top forms for social workers working with adults too. As a society are we mad or what?

I know that the increased use of computers has led to a decrease in jobs, but to overload a few with this bureaucracy is just total madness and for what point? How does it actually benefit the young person or older person? It doesn't give them better education. Getting a school for an alienated kid, or even a bit of teacher input, is a frustrating, and usually non-productive, exercise.

There are loads of duties that have been imposed on social

workers but when it comes to it there is often some kind of cop-out. I was recently working with a very alienated thirteen-year-old girl. She at times was as wild as an alley cat. I took her and her mum along to meet a child psychiatrist because I wanted to check out whether she was mentally ill or just the most amazingly negative manipulator.

She decided to play the psychiatrist up and became pretty abusive. She had done this several times to me in the past but I'd got through it. She was thirteen years old, and had had a horrible experience being abused by a neighbour, but should have been at school. She was out of control and needed sorting out. Now, wouldn't you think that it should be the responsibility of a psychiatrist to try to sort her out? Well, what happened was that the psychiatrist walked out of the room, leaving me and the mum with the alley cat. She said that she wasn't going to be talked to like that.

If social workers did that no one would ever get sorted out. We got a letter from the psychiatrist saying that her agency was unable to provide her with a service. So who was? Me, of course, the trained-to-be-an-expert-in-everything social worker.

I was the one who stood up in the magistrates' court to say that this was a bright kid who needed a second chance and could go to university one day. I was the one who gave her Phoebe's lucky bracelets to borrow to help her get through the experience and stop her from being detained. Of course, this sounds like I was the heroine. Well, in this case I was. I worked damned hard with her and her family, because – let's face it – who else was going to?

Christmases

You may wonder why I have a separate section for Christmases. Well, it's because I had four Christmases without the children. They went to stay with Tim. The first time that he mentioned it I began to panic and wondered how I would cope without them. But if you are separated and live a hundred and forty miles from each other these are the kind of decisions that you have to make. Many of my friends and work colleagues thought that I was mad but now that Tim is no longer alive I am so glad that they went. I want them to always remember their dad. Fortunately, Stephen feels very strongly that Tim was their dad and is happy for them and me to talk about him whenever we want.

So I spent four Christmases with my mum and dad. I would meet Tim at the Birmingham Rep for the Christmas Eve performance and then I would go home and the children would go to number 26. I would ring them several times while they were there. They usually stayed for a week.

The Dell would seem so quiet without them. It was nice spending time with Mum and Dad, playing Scrabble, but it would have been nice to have had a wild boozy time with a crowd of people. I have often dreamed of hiring a Scottish castle and having a crowd of people for Christmas. Maybe I'll get my dream one day – who knows?

The last Christmas was the best. I suppose I had come more to terms with it and could be a little more self-centred and indulgent. There was no one to see me eat chocolates and drink fizzy wine in the bath at a pretty early hour, and the walk home at 10.00pm from Mum and Dad's with a crisp, starry sky was so romantic. The problem was that I had no one to share it with.

Chapter 12 –
The New Millennium and Beyond

We spent New Year's Eve of the new millennium with Tim just outside York in a mobile home. The children had spent Christmas with him. They then went to collect the van and met me in the car park of Safeway in Newport. Tim wouldn't come to Gnosall – he said that he would never come here again. I think it was moving stuff to the first house that sealed it for him – he just found it too emotional.

We travelled through Derbyshire to Yorkshire. New Year's Eve in York was very disappointing as we found that there was nothing particular arranged. So we had a bottle of booze and watched the fireworks from the mobile home and then I went to bed rather grumpily. What a thrilling way to spend the end of two thousand years.

New Year's Day was much more fun. We drove to Scarborough and arrived just in time to see the New Year's Day bathers. Tim missed it because he was parking the van, but me and the children were lucky to see them take their freezing cold plunge.

I haven't written for several days. A kind of self-doubt in my own worth. Why should anyone want to read my story? Also, there are sad things happening in Stephen's family that make me want to cry but which don't belong to me so I can't share with you. That has been our story – a mixture of wonder, happiness and total sadness – but I'll now return to the beginning of 2001.

Tim used to love science fiction and the film *2001 – A Space Odyssey* was special to him and I suppose reaching the actual year 2000 was a bit weird. The same as getting past 1984 and all the other times when the world is supposed to come to an end. In January 2001 I didn't really know whether Tim and I had come to an end or not. I just carried on with life and the things I was supposed to do.

Pattern of work

By January 2000 Phoebe was nine years old and Josh was seven. They were both becoming anti-childcare. They just wanted to be able to play with their friends. I found a teenager, Mary, who was the daughter of a friend, who was keen to look after them and so I paid her to come to the house.

That year I worked until the end of March in a children and families team and then worked until July in an adults team. I enjoyed the contrasting work. I also had some students after April and found that I had little time at home but not the same kinds of financial rewards as working part-time.

I have always felt myself to be fortunate being both a mum and a part-time worker. Tim gave me £400 a month, which was enough to pay the mortgage and half of the bills, and so I didn't need to work full-time.

During this period I was interviewed by researchers twice for the government's research on childcare. I suggested that using teenagers was a good idea and that they should be rewarded by being given a National Insurance credit which could go in later life to their pension. I feel that the emphasis on childcare has always been on adults and that children's feelings are rarely taken into account.

My kids are lucky that they have always had good childcare. Perhaps not as stimulating as I might have liked, but certainly more than adequate. But they had been there, done that, and now just wanted to play with their mates.

So the year went on much the same as the last two, and then things began to change.

The chatroom

My excuse for going into an internet chatroom was that the children were busy playing and I had become the base to come to for regular check-ins, to be fed and occasionally for a different type of stimulation – I wasn't really a person in their eyes; just the controller. I had no money to enable me to go out and pay someone else to take on this role, so I just fell into the chatroom.

I tried the BBC ones but found them a bore, and then found Excite. My internet connection hadn't worked for a while, after I had dismantled the computer for Bonfire Night. It just didn't do anything – a perennial problem I have – and then I took the modem into a shop in Stafford, where it was sorted out fairly cheaply.

So I found Excite and started going in the forties room. It was always much busier in there than any of the other rooms. I must admit I gave up on many occasions through total boredom. I decided that the best thing to do was to ask people what they did and then if they did something interesting I would carry on talking to them. I did speak to a few women but I suppose it was much more fun talking to the blokes. Sometimes I would talk to five different blokes at the same time.

Whatever people say about chatrooms, you can be brash and brazen and really just have a good laugh, because ultimately it's just like the TV: you can switch it off and never have to go on it again.

I can't remember when I started in the chatroom. I think it was just before the summer holidays in 2000. Stephen was the second person I spoke to. I used the name Isissun, taking Phoebe's middle name of Isis and adding "sun" to get the required amount of letters. Well, I picked Stephen. I had to really, because he was Rameses. Two ancient Egyptian names, both very significant in their own right. So how could I not pick him?

I spoke to a psychic a few months ago, who told me that Stephen and I were related to each other in a previous life. It was strange because from the first time I heard his name I thought I knew him from somewhere.

I spoke to him once in the chatroom and we exchanged email addresses. I wasn't too interested in him because he had been a children and families team leader and was then an FE lecturer in caring. It was spookily close to what I had done. Until then I had always believed that it was healthier to be with someone whose work was very different from your own. Besides, he lived two hundred miles away in Gosport, so what was the point of getting to know him? So Stephen and I exchanged very occasional emails and I carried on tinkering and flirting with other people in the chatroom.

The one that really caught my eye was a guy called Alan, who lived in Walsall. Although he was an accountant, he worked with a lot of people in show business and he had been involved in getting some theatrical productions going. He sounded quite fun and so after several emails he rang me up and we started to talk to each other. By now it was about late November and we decided to meet up while the children were at Tim's, just after Christmas.

We had exchanged photographs and I knew that he was smaller than me, but I thought, so what?

Chatrooms always tell you about a load of safety stuff and I personally could never understand a lone person under the age of thirty, or a child, meeting up with someone, but for a person in their forties with kids, well, you can pace yourself and where else can you find someone interesting?

So I decided to meet up with Alan. We decided to meet in a pub near Telford so if we cowered out then we could just walk away. It was one of those kinds of ridiculous joke meetings. Little did I know that Alan's geography was worse than mine. I had acquired a mobile phone by now – having broken down twice with one child in the car and another time miles away – so Alan was able to ring me. I sat and waited and felt a bit like a tart waiting for a pick-up.

In fact, there was a very dishy-looking farmer in the pub who occasionally glanced in my direction. I did think that I might prefer to have a drink with him but then I am a loyal, committed person and so would never have let Alan down.

Well, eventually I got a call to say he was lost and after several other calls and trying to direct him, he said that he had found himself in Gnosall. I told him to stay put and went on an Alan hunt. I found him, got out the car and thought, "Oh my god, what have I done?" I realised that I was just as prejudiced as the next person. I didn't want a man smaller than me (Stephen is about seven inches taller than me).

We then decided to head off towards Haughton, the next village, and found that the pub I knew about had stopped serving meals, so we headed back to Gnosall. We ended up in a pub in Gnosall and I hoped that I wouldn't see anyone that I knew, as meeting Alan was a secret. I didn't really want anyone to know. We then went back to my house for a chat. By now I was quite ready to get rid of Alan but felt a bit sorry for the chaos.

It was an experience but one I didn't want to repeat. The last time I had been on a first date was when I was seventeen years old. I was now forty-five, so it was hard to know what you were supposed to do. Alan was more nervous than me though, and I don't know why, but second time around in many things in my life has been best.

A surprise visitor

Tim had always said that he would never come to Gnosall again. Well, it was my birthday. I was forty-five and I had gone out with the children somewhere. We arrived home about 9.15pm and I was just getting Josh off to sleep when there was a knock on his window. Living in a bungalow, this was from the back garden. We went to the window and there was Tim. Josh just shouted "Daddy!" and Phoebe, who was getting ready for bed, went charging through towards the back door, which we used as our main entrance.

It's strange that it was one of those occasions which you just don't expect. Phoebe was to be ten the next day and Tim had come for her birthday. Apparently, he had sat in the next road for over an hour waiting for us. It was a dreadful night, with torrential rain, and he said that he had nearly decided to go.

The children were absolutely over the moon but I just felt put out. I had always been so accommodating but now I felt that Tim was an intruder in my house. He had left it too long and I knew from that night that our relationship was finally over. However, it wasn't until Christmas Day that I finally took off my wedding ring for good.

Being nameless

I suppose perhaps I am a little strange, but getting married, to me, is about sharing the same name. I don't think that you have to take the bloke's name. I think you can choose, or even make up a new name if you prefer, but it's about having the same name. So when I felt that Tim and I were finally finished I began to think of who I was and then realised that I felt nameless. I continue with this feeling today.

Shakespeare said "That which we call a rose by any other name would smell as sweet" (Romeo and Juliet) – but would it?

My two names have always been difficult for other people to say and spell, so perhaps I am better off being nameless. Rachel Bramble is just a pen name. Through much of my career I have just been Rachel.

Chapter 13 – Facing the Truth

When I started writing chapter thirteen I was still with Stephen and very much in love with him. It was an obsessional kind of love where he was always in my head. I later learnt that the closeness I had with him was all a fake. Throughout our relationship he was seeing another woman, although until I threw him out in October 2002 she had very little time with him.

Looking back now, I realise how naïve I was but I don't regret my time with Stephen – it was a very good learning experience for me and I have come across lots of other women who are not so lucky. Whatever happened between us, Stephen encouraged me to write this book.

Losing Tim

For three years the children and I went on holiday to southern Spain during the February half term. The week before we went Tim rang to say that he had to go to hospital for some tests because he was having back problems.

When we returned from holiday he was still in hospital and he told me, through Dad, that he had cancer of the bowel. I suppose I, like everyone who hears the word "cancer", have visions of finding the sufferer dead the next day. You hear the word "prognosis" but in Tim's case it was anything between a few weeks and several years. It depended on his psychological state, we were told.

At the time, Dad had known about his cancer for about a year but was still very fit and to an outsider would appear to be a rather fit seventy-eight-year-old who was getting on with his life. Well, Tim died within seven weeks. The last time the children saw him he was all bent up and painfully thin, looking like an old man. He just wasn't Tim. The last time I saw him he wasn't too bad and even still had a sense of humour. I held his hand and wanted to give him a hug but felt that this was hypocritical. I wish I had now.

It was such a strange time. I was so in love with Stephen and yet so upset about Tim. Both were constantly in my thoughts and I cried and cried and cried. You hear of people dying from a broken heart, and when you have this level of emotional pain you can see how real this could be.

It's very hard to write about deceit and a broken heart but that was what I felt when I found that Stephen had been deceiving me for the whole time that I had known him.

Soon after I had met him I received a letter from a woman who said that she had been his partner for eleven years. I had just come back from a holiday with the kids in Spain. The whole time I had been there I had been thinking of Stephen and had been dying to see him again. When I arrived home there were three letters waiting for me, two from Stephen and one from the woman. I remember feeling sick when I opened and read the letter. My dreams were shattered. I rang Stephen and remember screeching down the phone at him. How could we possibly have any relationship? We got through it all and time went on. But always at the back of my mind was the doubt. She had said that Stephen was meeting both with me and another woman. He had been painted as an evil monster, which I know he is not.

As time went on, there were a couple of times when I had my doubts but when you really love someone and had lived the sheltered life that I had – remember that I hadn't dated since I was seventeen years old – you tend to put the thoughts of jealousy on yourself and justify them by saying that it must be the menopause.

When Stephen went for a trip down south in October 2002 I had an urge to look through a plastic bag and found a phone bill which used our old address. On the bill was the same number being phoned on a regular basis. My heart sunk – I knew that he had been ringing another woman and I just knew who she was.

This is the kind of situation that you read about in magazines and think that it won't happen to you. All sorts of emotions go on inside you but most of all there is an awful panic and feeling of sickness. How could he do it to me, you think.

I picked up the phone, dialled 141 and then the number. A woman answered the phone and I asked her if she had been ringing us. She didn't even know who I was but said that she must have got a couple of numbers wrong. I hung up and thought, What do I do now? Oh my God – it is true. Stephen had been deceiving me. I dialled again and she answered. I asked her how long my partner had been ringing her and she hung up.

I felt absolutely devastated. I called Stephen's phone and got the voicemail. I screamed down the phone that he was a total shit and how could he lie to me. I then sent him a text to say I never wanted to see him again and that all his things would be in the garage.

I was so angry and upset. I just felt betrayed. I sobbed my heart out and the children saw and knew everything straight away. I felt broken-hearted, devastated and just wanted to know why.

The next day was an exhausting packing of Stephen's things. The weather was bad and so a lot got boxed up to go into the garage. Both children helped with the packing but Josh was particularly brilliant. I forget how many times he went up to the local shop to bring home some more boxes.

When I spoke to Stephen a few days later he found it very difficult to talk and had sent me a few texts but the last said that he wasn't trying to avoid me, just that he couldn't face himself.

Friends and family were a wonderful support to me. I rang the other woman the day after I threw Stephen out and talked to her for about half an hour. Throughout the conversation she said that I should talk to Stephen about things. She said that she wanted to stay his friend and that she had told him that he needed to go away and sort out what he wanted for himself. I find it very difficult to imagine being in her position as the other woman. It feels as though I got the freshly prepared meal and that she got what was ready for the compost heap.

However, I cannot excuse Stephen. I found out that he had been seeing her the whole time that he had been with me. As I think of him now, I cannot believe that he is an evil monster. I believe that he was confused and guilt-ridden. Time does help and although I have been very disappointed I have learnt an awful lot from the experience.

Seeking Amazing

My antidote to worrying about Stephen was to join a dating agency; probably a daft thing to do but I thought, well, if I can get a few letters or emails it might distract me a little and stop me sending the endless texts to Stephen about worrying about him and the day-to-day going on.

I also thought that it would do him good not hearing from me because I know that he loves knowing what I am doing, and in fact this did have the right effect. It wasn't that I wanted Stephen back or that this was a form of revenge – it was just a distraction.

So I joined an agency which specialised in "green" people. I thought that I would be more likely to get someone a little more interesting than the characters who went to the chatroom. I wrote to a few men (we only had details of the opposite sex) and had a few okay replies. I then found the online version and emailed some of them too.

Then last Saturday, 16th November 2002, I found "Amazing".

I thought that this was an excellent way to finish this part of the book. But before I tell you about Amazing I will just say that yesterday, 22nd November, I saw Stephen again and we have started to evolve into our new roles. How they turn out is for a future book, but for now I will finish with Amazing as it permeates both me and what I want for the future.

I had emailed all of the people I thought looked interesting in the list of profiles and although I had a few "Hi there" replies, I was rather disappointed. I knew that my own profile would not be in the paper version until January 2003 and I was very impatient. If Stephen could have someone else, I wanted someone too. I wanted to see what it was like dating and had decided that perhaps I would go out with a few people rather than look for Mr Right.

I decided on the Saturday, after the kids had gone to bed, to just have another look. Well, the name Brian flew out at me because he said that he was a journalist and I thought, "Cor blimey, with all my interest in social work and the media." I had found my journalist. Could I possibly go out with a journalist?

So I emailed Brian. He had a picture of himself and looked okay for his fifty years. He was also six feet three inches tall and slim, but he lived in Peterborough. There was no reply, so I thought, "Oh well, never mind, it was worth a try," and I began to think once again that I had to accept a life on my own (a regular feeling that I get).

On Monday I got a text message to say that Brian had emailed me. Well, that was the beginning of Amazing and three of the greatest fun days of my life and a perfect antidote to Stephen. Brian said in his profile that he was not looking for ordinary, he was looking for amazing.

Brian and I had the most wonderful to-ing and fro-ing of texts and emails all day Monday, and then on Tuesday the texts were flying to such an extent that at one point I had to say Brian, "Look, I have to do some work." By Wednesday the texts had virtually disappeared and then on Thursday, after a long phone call on Wednesday night with possible plans to meet up, Brian told me that he was a complete fake and that I should not get involved with him as he had broken the hearts of fifteen women, only claiming originally to have had three in his life and that basically he was a miserable git who went from bar to bar pretending that he had friends. He said that he fell in love too easily and that already he had lots of women who wanted to meet up with him.

I really knew that he was a fake but he was a journalist and he could write. I suggested that we wrote a book together called *Seeking Amazing – The Social Worker and the Hack*. It would be about our lives and thoughts and I hope that I can coax him to stay in touch and do it. I also said that I would not meet with him until it was published and so I will leave you with Brian's definition of "Amazing":

"I want to be so much in love that I wake every morning with my heart zinging and a smile on my face. I want to walk down the street hand in hand with my partner feeling proud that she has chosen to love me. I want to have the most incredible sex time and time again, giving my partner orgasm after orgasm, each one more intense than the last (and vice versa). I want to share cold winter nights by the fire, drinking wine and talking and laughing. I want to feel as though I am in love for the first time again."

I close my eyes and just think, "Wow – so do I!"

Time goes on

Since finishing this part of the book life has moved on and there is a lot I could write about but I must stop for now as it is more important to get this out for the world to read.

Bureaucracy is going mad at the moment and so I must try to do something to stop this madness. The government talks about putting people first, but the systems it has created, and may continue to create, lessen the direct time that social workers have with their service users.

The fear of what might happen has led to a level of over-cautiousness which places names on the Child Protection Register where families should have received support, not the condemnation that having the label brings.

And so my personal life moves on. I wrote *Seeking Amazing*, but it now sits with my co-writer, probably collecting dust.

Happy endings/new beginnings

As my forty-eighth birthday looms, I suppose it's nice to tell the reader that I can report a happy ending or a new beginning.

For those who get the chance when it is published, read *Seeking Amazing* (co-written with Paul Nixon) – it is *amazing*, the people I came across over a six-month period of recording in detail my experience of internet dating and, yes, I found my Mr Amazing, the man who is so different from Stephen and who I am so happy just knowing, and the man who truly lets me dream once again and gives me all the love and cuddles that I will ever need, and most importantly just likes me to be me.

Part II – Ideas and Theories

I have hundreds of ideas but most I have to smother because they can just become overwhelming. Some have emerged and been used to some extent, but until now none of them have been published.

I am a dreamer, but as I get older I am becoming more of an activist. I don't believe that action is greater than words. I believe that they should complement each other and that action should be considered for the good of people not for the power of certain individuals.

I am also a storyteller – you give me three things and I will tell you a story. I think that it is good for the mind to drift into a story. This book is very much about me and why I am a social worker, and so included in Part II are some of my ideas about social work and tools that I think could help social workers be better at what they do.

What is the point of successive inquiries into child deaths pinpointing communication as central to the reason for failing to protect children if no one makes communication the most important part of the work and recognises that even the best communicators need to constantly sharpen their skills?

I find that all that pinpointing blame does on the whole is to lead to greater unrealistic and unmanageable accountability. Why have three forms when you only need one? Why have all the wonderful computer technology but then have mountains of paper?

Tim was a brilliant computer man and fifteen years ago he worked out simple systems that could have been used to link all the different agencies, and different levels of alert to show degrees of risk, but then I was a nobody and my ideas were to be humoured not considered.

Chapter 1
The flow of information

For some time I have been concerned about the amount of information that is dumped on people every day. There is a big difference between information that you choose and that which you are expected to know.

If I consider my own situation, as well as being a worker, I am a mum, a daughter, a girlfriend and a friend. In each of these roles I am expected to retain information. I couldn't live without my good old diary but what I feel is happening is that, due to the increasing amount of bureaucracy, an increasing amount of information is being created.

In lots of ways it isn't the amount that is the problem; it is how it is distributed and the impact of that distribution. I had an example of this at work just the other day when I was preparing a report for a child protection conference. I asked my boss and colleagues what format I should use and there was confusion about which was the right one as several were floating around the office. This is concerning because in most of the inquiries that happen after child abuse deaths it is found that the communication between the professionals has been poor. I increasingly encounter the "It's not our responsibility" attitude.

Three different types of flow of information are described below, along with the probable consequences in each of the styles. The models are applied specifically to social work but could be used in a number of organisations.

Top down

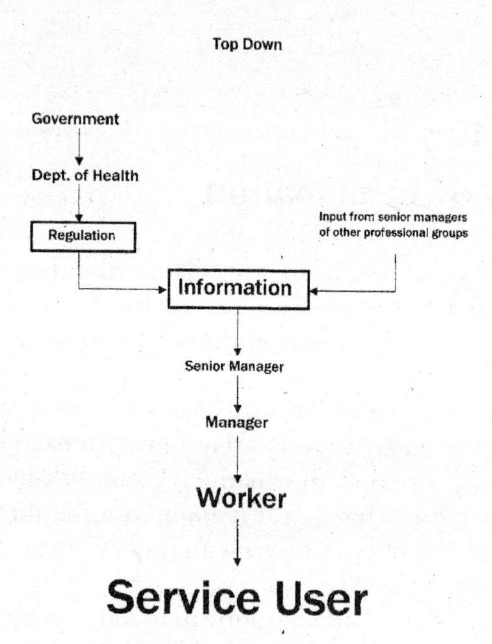

In the top down model information is received at the top by the senior managers, who then sift the information and decide what should be passed to the managers and give guidance on what should be distributed to both the social workers and the service users.

The advantage of this model is that there is a form of selection process and so people lower down the tiers are not bombarded with information. The disadvantage is that information only flows from the top down, with a lack of useful information being passed up and within tiers. Also, if applied to a larger structure, such as information being passed from the Department of Health, the meaning of the information can be distorted on the way. This model does not have built-in mechanisms for feedback and so allows the senior managers at the top to become distant from the service users at the bottom.

A current example of how this model is not working in the childcare field is the use of Action Assessment Records, which were devised to help looked-after children have a better quality of life but are often seen as irrelevant by the young people themselves. Social workers are pestered to get young people to complete them and records of completion rates are returned to the Department of Health, but these records don't seem to allow for comments on why they didn't complete them by either social workers or service users.

Another example of this is the completion of Core Assessments, which only show a snapshot in time of a child's life circumstances. In the period from writing this book to publication and beyond there will be numerous new pieces of information flowing from the top, but the problem is what happens if suddenly the senior managers realise that there was information that should have been passed down but wasn't or that should have been passed upwards?

Blocked sink effect

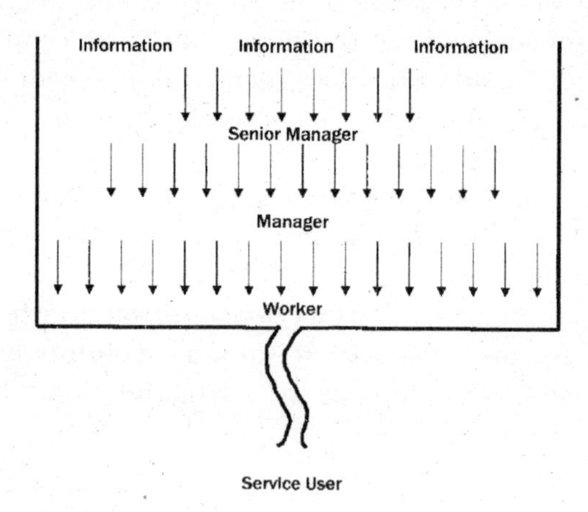

With the blocked sink effect, information is passed from the top through the managers and heads towards the social workers and the service users. The quantity of the information is not controlled and as it reaches the bottom there is a build-up, as in a blocked sink. At some point or other the plug is pulled out and a lot of old, out-of-date and useless information is passed through. As with the blocked sink, this can be dangerous, because if the information gets into the wrong hands it can lead to confusion.

This happened recently when I tried to find out which form I should use to make a referral to a psychologist. I rang the department to ask what was happening to support a family, only to find that I had sent the form to the wrong place because it had been sitting in the drawer and, being a newcomer to the office, I assumed it was the right form. In this particular case it wasn't a life and death situation, but it could have been.

I suspect that if this model was used in the inquiries of several of the child deaths, the stagnant water of the blocked sink could represent the blocking of information.

So what is the ideal flow of information? The answer to this is sifted free flow.

Sifted free flow

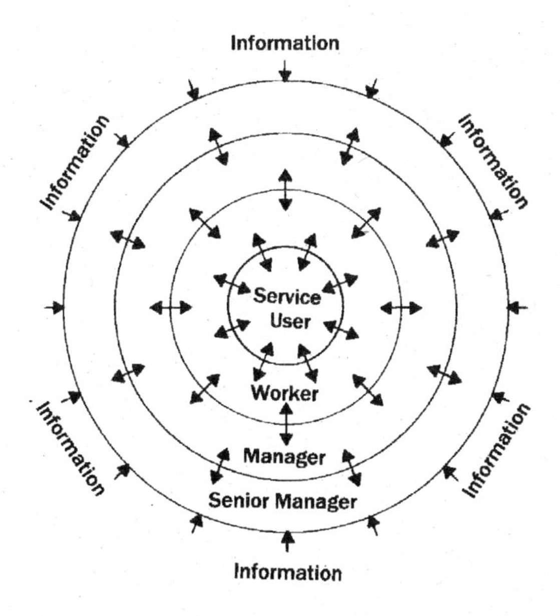

In the sifted free flow model everyone is taught about the importance of information and what kind of information is required, in what circumstances, and how to present it in a clear and concise way. People are also taught how to question and ask for clarification. This is important because of cultural and individual meanings.

Free flow cannot be taught in a day and everyone concerned has to be constantly alert. It is important that all professionals take responsibility in this model. If they don't then it is easy to be taken over by the blocked sink effect. To get a real understanding of the complex nature of the information refer to "Communication awareness" below.

In the sifted free flow model information flows in all directions through the different people concerned. Also, more imaginative methods of information are used. This is a confident use of information and the key sifters need to be there to encourage the flow rather than increase or decrease it through misplaced power.

Sifted free flow is based on a philosophy of achieving the best for the service user but with an understanding of everyone concerned. To be a successful sifter you may benefit from becoming more open and aware of all elements of communication.

Chapter 2
Communication awareness

I have been concerned for some time that every time there is a child death followed by an inquiry, the most common explanation for things going wrong is poor communication between the professionals involved in the case and/or members of the public.

This is not an academic book and so I have no intention of looking at individual cases. Instead I decided some years ago to actually look at the different elements of communication and see how they all fit together. I wanted to try to develop a working tool that could be used with all service user groups. A kind of universal toolkit. I have used this with several of my students and it has been interesting to see the students who have taken on board elements of it and come back with explanations of why things went well or badly.

The original idea of communication awareness came from the journalists' use of "who, what, where, when, how" – and I added "why". (Please refer to the descriptions of each element below.)

There are certain elements that I feel are underplayed by social work, in particular where and when. I feel that venues can have an importance in how we engage with and progressively work with our clients. I swing between "service user" and "client" because I really don't like either of the terminologies. Stephen really dislikes the terminology "service user" because a client to him relates to business and perhaps solicitors. To me it conjures up thoughts of prostitutes.

This is the fickle thing about working with people: our understanding and interpretation of the world. Communication awareness does not impose a vision of the world; it just gives guidance on areas of people's lives that make them who they are. Conflicts can be caused by all sorts of misunderstandings and differing expectations.

I had a childhood where the family on my mum's side all hugged and kissed each other when they met, but on my dad's side didn't. To me as a child this was quite confusing. Some families share out all the food for a meal, whereas others give some and then expect people to ask for a second helping. If you are used to the former you find that even if you haven't had enough it is difficult to ask for a second helping. If you are used to the latter you find it hard to eat the whole meal and at the end of it feel totally stuffed or sick. This happened with Tim's family, who shared out the meal, but I had been taught to eat everything off my plate.

People are immensely complicated and the social worker's role is to try to measure a balance between what is expected by society and by the service users. Communication awareness is a checklist. It's a kind of "By the way, have you thought of..."

An area which I have become increasingly interested in is the impact of smells. My mum always groans when I go on about smells, but if you talk to any social worker they will know people who live in houses that always have nasty stagnant smells.

We, of course, are all brought up with a sensitivity to people and so we won't go into someone's house and say, "Cor blimey! It doesn't half pong in here," but I bet if you are honest you often think it and the first thing you'd really like to do is open a window for a good old-fashioned blow through.

Very recently I was talking to a colleague at work about how nowadays I didn't hate ironing so much and wondered whether it was because I was using a perfumed liquid in the steam iron. We considered how different aromatherapy oils put in a steam iron could create different mood states. I haven't tried it yet but probably will some day.

Communication awareness is about looking at the relationships between people. It is about realising that people and their situations are constantly changing and it is about the impact of power and who has that power.

The diagrams below have stayed much the same for several years and given the time and energy could probably fill a book in their own right, but for now I shall leave them as they are to enable the publication of this book.

I hope that perhaps by using them you can see why tragedies such as the death of Victoria Climbié happened.

Guidance on the use of communication awareness worksheets

Users have the seven sheets to enable quick reference. The aim is to develop a working tool, which can be as simple or as complex as the user wants to make it. The worksheets can also be used in any social work setting and so enable transfer of already gained knowledge from one setting to another. Communication awareness can also be used to learn how to communicate on an interpersonal level, in group settings or in the wider multidisciplinary settings.

This introduces the six interrelated aspects of communication: who, why, what, where, when and how. It also considers issues of power and oppression, whether obviously displayed or latent through misguided goodwill. For example, the production of the AARs (Action Assessment Records) by the Department of Health may have genuinely been conceived as a tool to help looked-after children, but has in fact turned out to be rather oppressive.

This also considers people as *thinking* people, with their own ideas about life.

Communication Awareness

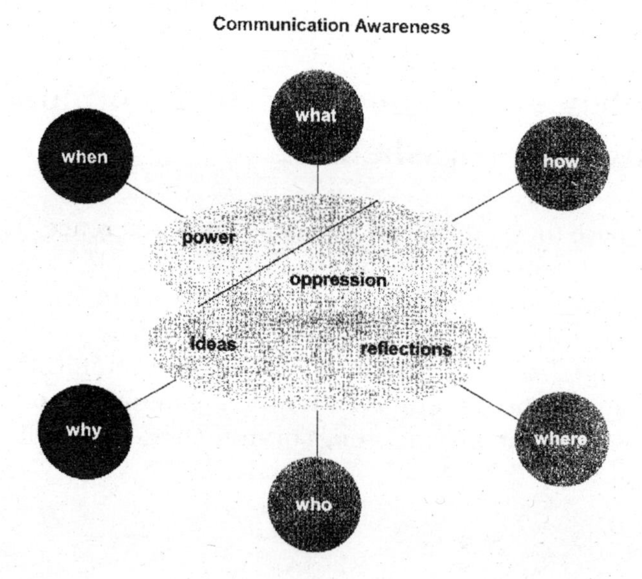

Who

"Who" considers the relationship between self (me), positive warm relationships, which can be personal or professional (you), and the more distant and possibly conflicting relationships (them).

It considers the many aspects that affect these relationships, to include areas that are not often considered, such as personality traits and loyalties. Issues of power also affect all of the aspects. Each of these aspects could be explored more deeply. They can be used to look not only at why things went well in a given situation, but also why they may have gone badly. For example, were there differing assumptions about an action taken?

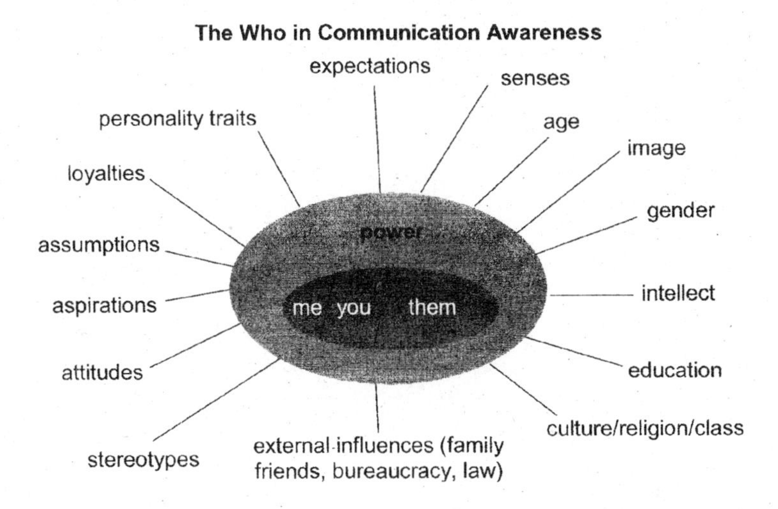

Why

"Why" considers why we communicate. It may seem simplistic, but how often do workers actually think about why they are doing things; and do we communicate better when we want to or when we are told to? These are areas that we should continuously consider.

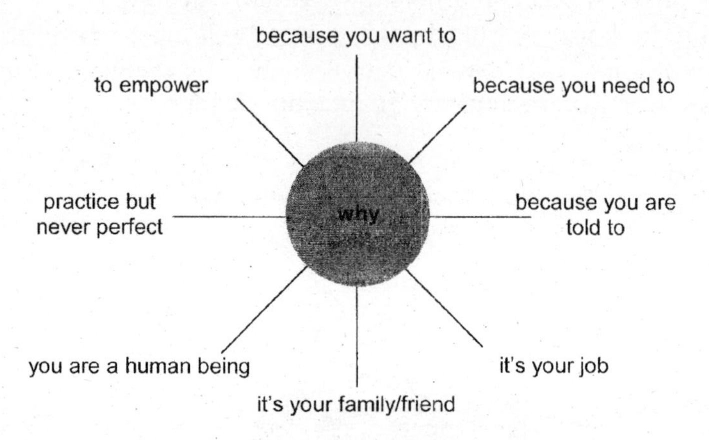

What

"What" considers what we communicate. I always emphasise encouragement and praise, both on a human level and as a way of improving productivity.

Social Services are generally poor at praising good work. We do not have award ceremonies like the media and I think perhaps that we should. Perhaps you could encourage industry to award us – I'm sure a few choccie bars would go down well. How do we communicate about something we don't believe in or don't agree with? For example, if we have to gather information that we feel is irrelevant, how do we justify the need to do this?

I am constantly reminding colleagues that when we train as social workers we do not train to be a social worker for a particular authority or organisation – we are training to be social workers for *society* and for individuals in society and if there are things that we are told to communicate about that we don't agree with, our consciences should challenge this, otherwise we could end up like the German people under Nazism or other, more modern-day, oppressive states.

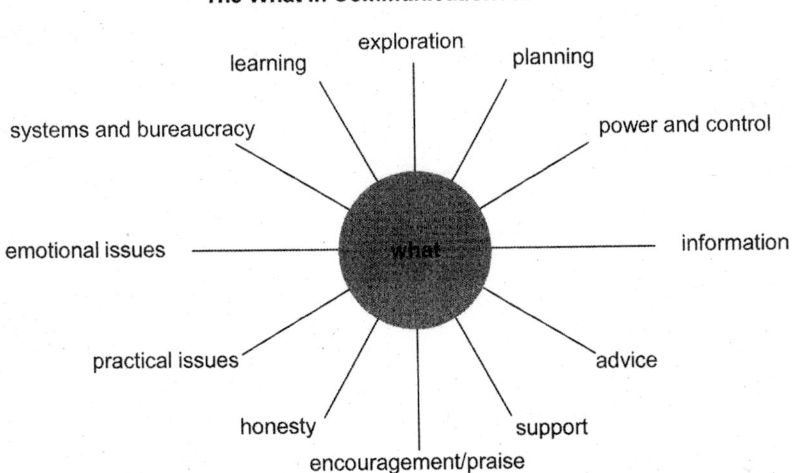

Where

Often venues, and their potential impact on the effectiveness of communication, are not thought about. Where considers the elements that could affect communication, including aspects such as "smells".

In private many social workers would admit that many of their dysfunctional families live in properties where a window is never opened and the stagnant smells seemed to have reflected the occupants' lives. I think that there could be a very interesting study carried out in this area, particularly in relation to depression and general mental health.

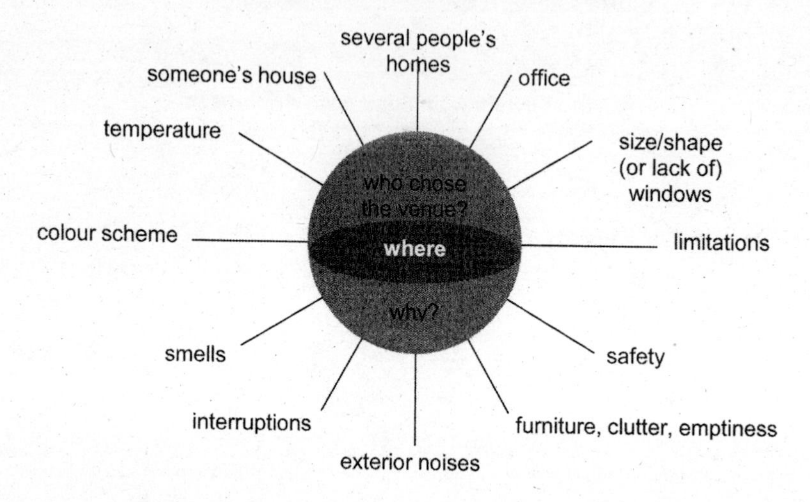

When

"When" considers the time of day and day of the week, and the power relations in terms of time. What is quite important is teaching students about length of meetings.

I once observed a student with a service user who was on a hospital ward and very poorly. After he introduced himself, he said that he wouldn't stay very long. Forty-five minutes later I had to intervene, as the poor elderly person had certainly had enough and the student appeared unaware. This was particularly disconcerting as he was a second-year student. These kind of things may be obvious to many of us but I'm afraid not all.

Conversely, if you are undertaking a detailed assessment, it cannot be carried out in ten minutes. I try to get students to empathise with the service user and the importance of the service user's time.

The When in Communication Awareness

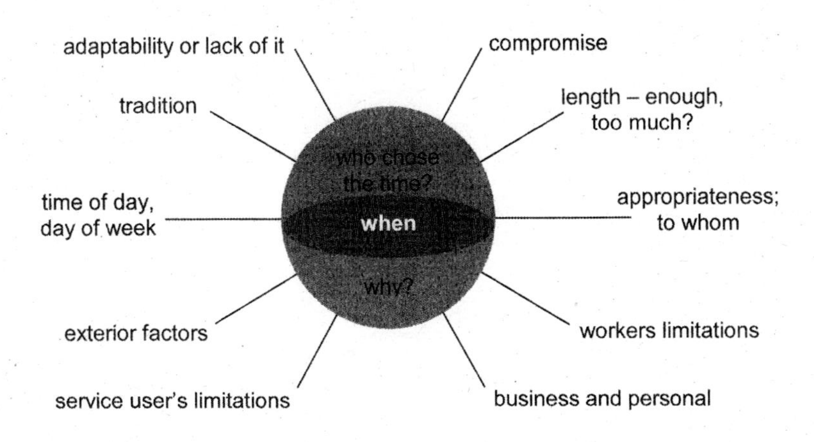

How

"How" looks at some of the methods used for communication. Students are encouraged to add extra ideas to the sheets of aspects, which I may not have considered.

Note that this material is my original work and has never before been formally published. I originally designed and produced communication awareness in 1998 and I have used it with all of my social work students since that date.

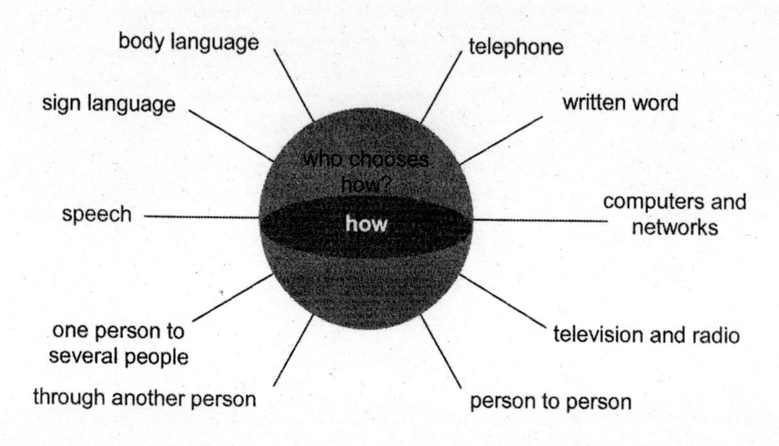
The How in Communication Awareness
body language
telephone
sign language
written word
who chooses how?
speech
how
computers and networks
one person to several people
television and radio
through another person
person to person

Chapter 3
The mouse and the lion – the relationship between social work and the media

I have been a qualified social worker for over twenty years. When I completed my training in 1982 I was concerned about the growing power of the media and the generally poor image of social workers.

It is appalling to find that twenty years on there are still a significant number of people who believe that social workers simply snatch children and take them into care, or fail to protect children. The ignorance of the public is perpetuating this image.

I believe that the reason for this lies in the fact that the public do not have more than a glimpse of social work through the media. Can you remember the last time you saw a social worker on TV and, if you were fortunate enough to see one, were they like anyone that you know?

The last one I saw was in a drama called *The Cry*. It was a good bit of drama but when the social worker spent all night observing suspected abusers on a hospital ward. I thought, "Oh, come on scriptwriters, get real." She also had a father who was a Cabinet Minister with easy access to the PM. And guess what? Yes, she ran off with the baby at the end of the first part. Of course, I had to see the second part to see what happened next. It just got more and more ridiculous.

If social workers were on TV every day, like the police, doctors and nurses, this representation would be okay. The public would have knowledge of different types of social workers. Currently, however, we get so little coverage and so it is rather worrying.

I believe that I have the answer to why social work gets so little coverage and if we can get to grips with my diagnosis then we could change our position forever. If we don't, then we will just have to accept all that is done to us and fear for our service users.

I believe that social work is organisationally introverted and the media is organisationally extroverted. This does not mean that all people who work for either of the organisations have these traits, but that the majority do, and if they don't there is an expectation to conform to the traits. Generally, the people that have the traits are the front people. In the case of social work it is the social workers and, in the case of the media, the journalists and TV/radio presenters.

In social work we have structures that are dominated by different forms of accountability. We have become so inward-looking and concerned about making sure that we follow correct procedures that we have forgotten our roots, our desire to improve the quality of life for all our service users.

What is the point of having children looked after if we have to keep moving them around the country from one placement to the next. We get caught up in the difficulties in terms of the paperwork, the timescales and the increasing costs, and we forget how they must be feeling.

We have multidisciplinary working, but often this ends up as a battleground for whose responsibility it is to do the sorting out. Working with older people in a hospital setting can make you want to pull your hair out, and when things go right there is just a feeling of relief.

We should be being creative, working with our service users to discover what's best for them. Of course, initiatives like listening to children are important. However, children should be guided by us, not dictating to us. We should be honest with them about the "real" world, otherwise we set them up to fail like their parents did before them. Giving a fifteen-year-old looked-after child £40 a month to go to a gym is not going to help her when she has to live off £42 a week in benefits.

We have become trapped by our introversion and it's time to learn from the media. It's time that we began to sing our own praises. It's time that we stopped taking all the burdens of society on our shoulders. It's time to be honest with the public about the difficulties we are having, and the only way to do this effectively is to start looking more outwardly by being honest about our relationship with the media. If we don't do this then eventually we will be replaced.

To explain the relationship I will use the metaphor of the mouse and the lion, with social work as the mouse and the media as the lion. I suspect that some readers have had pet mice, which they have enjoyed and have fond memories of, but generally mice are seen as vermin, rather smelly and breeding very quickly. They also are supposed to squeak and scurry away, quickly hiding in certain spaces. There are, of course, smart mice like Jerry, from the *Tom and Jerry* cartoons, but generally speaking people don't want mice around. There is also an image of people being frightened of mice, with women standing screaming on chairs. The image of social workers could thus be seen as the mice.

Over the last twenty years social workers have grown in number but they haven't grown in confidence. If we had, why would we accept begrudgingly all the paperwork that is often repetitive and under-utilised? For those of you in childcare, think of the LAC documentation. Do you really get young people to complete the Action Assessment Records? Do you know who produced them? And do you know that each one costs about £17? As a taxpayer do you really approve of money being spent that way?

Social work, as an organisation, is rather oversensitive and concerned about what it does and what people think about it. How many social workers are expected to take a complaint form out with them on a first visit to a service user? Would a journalist do the same? I doubt it. But we do, although we know that what we do is the best we can with the resources that we have.

If social workers are asked what they do, they tend to hide away, saying that they couldn't possibly tell because it is confidential, but in reality they could tell a great deal without disclosing personal information. Think how students write their competencies or case studies, referring to scrambled letters of real service users.

We are so introverted that we are unable to challenge. We cannot ask questions like, why does it cost £350 a week to look after an older person in a nursing home and £3500 to keep a child in a private children's home? What we do know is that when we find what we regard as a good placement for a child, even if it's a hundred miles from their home town, and they are happy there, after a few weeks we are requested by our managers to bring them home because, however good the placement is, it costs too much. We submit, feeling sad and disgruntled.

Why don't we tell our MPs about our difficulties? They are our representatives and are being funded by the public through taxation the same as we are. I suspect the answer is that our introversion takes over and we become fearful for our jobs.

The image of the media, on the other hand, is extroverted and most of the public media – i.e., the people that the public see, hear or read – display an outgoing, forceful image. Along with this image is the need to have answers now; not tomorrow or next week, but now.

How many of our service users try to adopt this "instant service" stance, causing chaos in Social Services reception areas all over the country by swearing, shouting, thumping furniture and making all sorts of threats when their needs aren't dealt with immediately?

The media is very good at self-praise, to the extent that it can bore the public with an array of award ceremonies for all sorts of occasions. It likes to regard itself as King of the Jungle and the leader, making statements and judgements, or deliberately trying to have a superior impartiality.

It is the trendsetter and fashionable – this means that there is a desire to join the lion's den and become a cub, which has been shown by the many thousands of people who try to get on programmes such as *Pop Stars* and by the boom in all types of media courses. When the lion roars, the public respond, and the lion is able to pick and choose who it wants in the den. This includes the people who work for it.

The lion can also be cruel, persecuting its victims. Think of how the different members of the *Big Brother* house were attracted to the lion's den, only to find themselves mutilated by the lion and thrown back to the outside world. They will probably be pulled back into the den at a later date so that the public can be entranced by what has happened to them since.

Who knows what happens to staff that don't conform to the image of the organisation?

Day-to-day social work is not seen as exciting enough for the hungry media. The hungry lion likes its meat to be rare and raw, of an earthy nature, and not well past its sell-by date and full of air. This means that because social work has so many hurdles to go over before they can approach the media, the media isn't interested. Social work cannot usually provide the media with earthy instant gratification and so the media is generally not interested in social work's "airy-fairy" approach.

The negative traits of the media (loudness, shallowness, insensitivity to individuals' feelings) and those of social work (oversensitivity, defensiveness, dithering and lack of assertiveness) mean that any form of mutual electricity is rare and short-lived. If the media shows any kind of interest beyond a fleeting glimpse, the mouse that is social work scurries away. If social work tries to approach the media, the lion shows a degree of sleepiness and boredom in the lack of meat that social work has to offer.

Usually two negatives can create a positive charge, but to do this there has to be some form of conductor and this usually only happens when lightning strikes, in the unfortunate death of a protected child. This charge wakes up the lion, who decides that the mouse is worth pursuing, until the charge disperses and the lion is no longer interested.

For social work and the media to live in harmony with a mutual duty to get the best for the people they both serve, there needs to be a period of taming and training. The hungry lion needs to be tamed to realise that meat can be just as good in different forms. The mouse needs to learn not to always scurry away but to stay put and pester the lion.

Both social work and the media need to understand their negative traits, because if they don't the lion will have to face another predator and the mouse will be squashed and destroyed forever.

Increasingly we see the privatised provision of services, which is expensive and far less value for money than the in-house equivalents. The private sector chooses the child or older person they wish to house, or dictates a price and numerous conditions to house the person. The local authority facility cannot do this. How often have you found children sleeping on settees in local authority homes because there is nowhere for them to go? The exhausted social worker cannot just go home – a child has to go somewhere.

But we don't tell the media this, and why not? Because our introversion makes us believe that it is our fault. We should have managed the budget better. Why can't we look for more investors like the media does? If we have a growing private sector, why are we constrained by public money, unable to get top-ups from local companies to improve our in-house facilities? Our introversion has made us reactive rather than proactive. I suspect that if all social care legislation were examined thoroughly, it would be found to have come about through failures rather than seeking success.

If you look on the politics website, ePolitix, you will find twice as many references to football than social work. That could be interpreted in one of two ways: either we are doing a good job or we are just not as important as football. Our introversion would claim the latter.

Social work and the media both need the public. Without the public our purpose doesn't exist and whether it is introverted social workers or the extroverted media is irrelevant. Social work is accountable to the public through the public purse. The media is generally accountable either through the public purse (in the case of the BBC) or through advertising revenue.

The meeting ground for both social work and the media is through education. The lion cannot live on meat alone and likewise the mouse cannot live just on scraps. Both need water to live and if they could meet at the watering hole of the oasis, perhaps in time they could drink next to each other, sharing the fresh taste and breathing the same air.

There are good things about being both an introvert and an extrovert, which can benefit the public. If social work and the media could try to learn from each other, using their positive traits, then the public could benefit too. If the media learnt to listen more, then when they want more variety of stories social workers may be encouraged to share. Likewise, if social workers stopped hiding behind confidentiality, they could share scenarios, learn to scramble identities and yet still provide interesting storylines.

If this could happen, the public would receive more variety from the media and social work would have greater status in society. Perhaps the media would then include social workers in local community awards and ask our advice to improve the content of their programme making.

From a personal perspective, I have made a start. I acknowledge my natural introversion and just the idea of trying to get this book published frightens me. I am not an academic and I am in awe of more fluent writers, but I feel that I have to bring out the positive qualities of my introversion my sensitivity, my desire to help the less fortunate in society, to tell the truth – all those attributes that have been rubbished and relegated to the "uncool" pile.

In February 2002 I wrote to all MPs about helping to build a better relationship between social work and the media. Of the hundred and fifty-nine who replied, seventeen didn't even think that social work was in their remit and hid behind parliamentary protocol – fortunately they weren't Cabinet or Shadow Cabinet members. Two weeks after I wrote, Tony Blair invited a group of social workers to tea at 10 Downing Street. This, of course, could be a coincidence, but it would be nice to think that it wasn't.

I have sent an outline of a proposal to include working with the media in the new social work course to the chair of the Health Select Committee, who is a former social worker. I am currently planning to contact a number of people known to the media and, with the help of my partner, I am starting a website dedicated to building this relationship.

If social work starts to understand its introversion, then hopefully it can also try to understand why the media shows little interest and, in time, use the media's positive traits to the benefit of the people we all serve, enabling a greater quality of life for many.

Maybe some day we will have a PQ in working with the media and then we can really get the stories we want to see into the media regularly.

I have left this unedited as it is trapped in the passion and time when it was written and there is a great temptation to give in to my natural introvert traits and make it less impassioned.

In July 2003, when I started proofreading The Nameless Social Worker, *I worked with a six-year-old child whose mother, two years before, had asked for assistance to help her find time to kick a drug problem. She voluntarily placed her child in the care of the local authority (now the looked-after system). During a period of ten weeks this child had three placements with three lots of foster parents. He had a tendency to run away and can you blame him? He just wanted to be with his mum and I was so glad the day that he, his foster parents (of two weeks) and his mum sat down for a celebratory breakfast at my suggestion because he was going home. I just hope that he and she get the support to keep him there.*

Chapter 4
Collaboration

Collaboration was written as an attempt to get an original script on TV. In 2000/2001 I attended a scriptwriting course on a weekly basis based at Keele University. It was an opportunity to learn through experience. We were all expected to be writing during the course. We would take in our writing to read out in the group. We would then comment on contributions. *Collaboration* was the first script I had written as an adult. As a child I had written scripts but I had always thrown them away as not good enough. I wish I had kept some as I would have loved to have had some to read today.

Episode One – Me, You and Them

By Rachel Bramble

Cast in order of appearance
Robot Lively – a marque II model
Joshua – a man in his mid-forties at the beginning of the story
Vicky – Joshua's partner, also in her mid-forties
Simon – the editor
Mark – a reporter
Peter – social work lecturer
Jane – social worker
Kate – social worker
Bob – a reporter aged eighty-two and sixty-two
Ted Malcolm – a man in his early fifties
Social workers and reporters – non-speaking parts

Scene one

A space age bedroom with lots of gadgets. A woman and a man are asleep. A robot enters the room

Robot Lively
Good morning Vicky and Joshua. It is nine o'clock precisely on a sunny day on the 28th August 2021

I have brought you the latest advertisement

Joshua
Oh Lively go away… it's too early to start looking at ads… we need to have time to wake up

Vicky
Looking directly at Joshua

You chose him Josh

Joshua
Well… Daisy was so drab and boring… I thought Robot Lively sounded much more fun for us

Vicky
Lively, come here. We might as well see the ad

Robot Lively
But if you're not in the mood then I'll leave it till later

Joshua
Oh no… not only lively… but we have a robot who goes into the grumps

Vicky
Show us the advert then Lively

Robot Lively puts the advertisement on. You see an elderly woman dressed up like Madonna and a man as a cartoon character

Advertisement dialogue
Welcome to TV Dementia Care, giving a total experience for your ageing relative.

You will have peace of mind, they will get pleasure in a virtual world reliving the most important times of their life. This leads to improved health and a longer life. Bring your relative to sample the delights of TV Dementia Care.

Helen likes to be Madonna and Bob really enjoys being cartoon characters.

The joint experiences of a couple with a vision, one a social worker, the other a journalist brought you the experience and a new world, a happy world of TV Dementia Care.

Come today and you will be happy tomorrow…

Joshua
Switch it off Lively

Robot Lively switches it off

Vicky
It's getting there but it's still a bit…

She pulls a face

Joshua
No... not quite right yet. You know, we've been working on this for seven years now

Vicky
What are you saying, are you not happy?

Joshua
Oh nothing

Vicky
Tell me

Joshua
I just remembered, that's all

Vicky
What, what did you remember?

Joshua
Twenty years ago, when we first met, what a different world it was then. Were we happier then than now?

Vicky
I don't think so, it was just a very different time... things have moved on. There was a lot of anger and prejudice... our two worlds were so separated. Your working world of social work was riddled with poverty, public ignorance and uncertainty. My world of the media was cocky, publicly so sure of itself, privately uncertain.

No Josh. It wasn't a happier time then; it was just different.

Just think how we used to live... in a time of the present, not thinking of our own future where we would need you and other social workers to care for us. We just wanted a story... getting the story was the important thing but your lot wouldn't give us the story.

No Josh, it was just a different time, a very different time

Joshua
He looks at Vicky with a serious expression

But... are we doing the right thing... shouldn't people live in the real world? That's what we thought then

Vicky
But Josh, what was the real world... sitting for hours in a chair... waiting for the next meal. We changed all that... we made people happy... they could choose to live today or yesterday... we just helped their memories

Joshua
He has a worried look on his face

But was it right?

Vicky
People wanted it

Joshua
But did they really... or was it you lot... the media telling them that that was what they wanted

Vicky
Oh Josh... I thought that we got over that blame many years ago... I thought we decided to work together to fight the prejudices and the ignorance... to tell the truth

Joshua
But what is the truth?

Vicky
We are the living truth. Can you remember when we first met, at the conference?

Joshua
Yes, I never really knew why you went there. Why did you go to the conference?

Vicky
One morning my boss called me to the office.

End of scene

Scene two

A busy office. Sitting behind a large desk is a man aged about forty. There is a knock on the door

Simon
Come in Vicky

Vicky enters the room

Vicky
You wanted to see me Simon

Simon
Yes. I've got a job for you, but I'm afraid nobody else wanted it and I thought that you'd like the experience

Vicky
What is it?

Simon
There's a conference being run by some social workers. It's to do with working with the media. They want to try to improve their public image.

Vicky
What kind of angle do you want me to get?

Simon

Well... really whatever you can get... they are getting a bit edgy at head office. We're supposed to get on with them but... well some of the crap they come out with they really need to get a life.
See what you can do. I'm planning it for page nine so it's low priority... just have a good lunch and mingle... you might find something...

I promise to give you Crown Court next week... the Tomms case is due to be tried.

Vicky

Simon, you promised me the Malcolm case but you gave it to Dave

Simon

Well you were doing a good job with the school inspection and Dave was available.

He moves towards her

If only you'd relax a little, you're too tense.

Vicky moves away from him. The phone rings; Simon picks it up

Not now Lorraine... I told you I was busy. Tell him I'll call him back.

He puts the phone down and moves towards Vicky again

Where were we... Oh yes

A young man bursts into the room

Mark
In an excited voice
There's a siege at Kingsway GNB... one confirmed dead... It's mine isn't it Si?

Simon
to Vicky
Do your best. We'll talk later

Vicky leaves the room

Now Mark, take George, and make sure you get some close-up shots of the family, especially the kids

Vicky looks behind her

Vicky
Angrily talking to the air
Bloody typical

End of scene

Scene three

Back in Vicky and Joshua's bedroom. Both are still in bed

Joshua
That Simon bloke really treated you badly... sounds as though he was a brute... the women in my office wouldn't have put up with that

Vicky
Well we knew that you either got on through sheer determination and a load of good luck or, well, you know what I mean... there was no way that I was going to let that creep dominate me. I saw too many women who were flavour of the month and then suddenly disappeared

Joshua
No wonder you became disillusioned

Vicky
Don't forget you did too

Joshua
I know but for totally different reasons... and I lasted a lot longer than you did

Vicky
I know... don't rub it in

Joshua
This is our time, our lie-in. I don't want to argue with you

Vicky
You never did… you were just like the rest of them… always wanting to keep the peace… avoiding aggro at all costs

Joshua
You talk as though we were a breed

Vicky
In a jokey voice

Well you were, weren't you?

Enter Robot Lively

Robot Lively
I heard an argument… should I activate a peace… under section 5b subsection 3 of the household rights… quote, if an argument does commence another should intervene

Vicky and Joshua
Oh go away Lively, not now

Robot Lively
Section 22 also says…

Joshua
Please Lively… go away, we are fine

Robot Lively
I was only trying to help

Vicky
If you don't go now... I'll pull the D switch

Robot Lively
In a grumpy tone

I'm turning off my audio receptor... goodbye

Exit Robot Lively. Joshua and Vicky hug each other and burst out laughing

Joshua
Looking at Vicky with an embarrassed expression

Don't you dare say a word

Vicky just laughs and laughs, then they both laugh

Joshua
You remind me of Kate at the conference. It was supposed to be a serious business but well she just...

Sadly

Remember what happened to her?

Vicky
Yes... she was very misunderstood

Joshua
But she still had a great sense of humour. She saw the funny side to things

Vicky
But it was no use in the end

Changing the subject

Do you remember Bryan? We used to make fun of him

Joshua
Yes… He was what people used to joke about, he had the beard and wore the Jesus sandals

Vicky
Didn't he also drive a 2CV?

Joshua
No, he had a Skoda

They look at each other and laugh

Joshua
The conference was intended to be a serious business. Most people were really committed. We wanted to change our image

Vicky
Sarcastically

You mean, you needed to change your image

Joshua
Yes, we did. People were suffering because they wouldn't come to us because of who they thought we were.

Don't you remember the discussion in the workshop where we met. It was about understanding each other

Vicky
And Kate stirred it up from the beginning

End of scene

Scene four

A room with some chairs in a circle. A man sits nervously in one of the chairs. Enter two women

Peter
Welcome

Jane
Is this "Understanding Each Other"?

Peter
Yes, I'm Peter Jones the facilitator for this group

They sit down next to each other and start whispering to each other.

More people enter the room in ones and twos. Vicky and Joshua enter at different times; all the twelve seats are filled up. Vicky sits next to Peter

Peter
Nervously

Well at least we've got some people who want to take the conference seriously. I believe that we have three journalists in our group. It's good to have you here

Enter Kate

Kate
Sorry I'm late Pete. I got lost

An extra chair is found for her, shuffling everyone around

Peter
Never mind, you are here now

Kate
In a sarcastic tone

I hope we're going to have a bit of fun

Peter
Ignoring Kate

It would be helpful to find out who everyone is and what their particular interest is in relation to understanding each other. I'm Peter Jones and I am a social work lecturer and part-time consultant, my speciality is working with older people.

Kate
Well, we could have a whole conference talking about the image of older people.

Peter
Yes Kate, I totally agree but that will have to be on another occasion

Kate
But surely we have to start somewhere, look at the way that the media generally portrays older people. I know that I work with children and families but my mother gets very annoyed

Peter
Ignoring Kate again, looking towards Vicky who is sitting next to him

Would you like to tell us who you are and why you are here?

Kate
Looking at Peter, sarcastically

This is the bit where we all forget who we are and what we do

Joshua
Sitting next to Kate, in a whisper

Kate, give it a rest

Looking towards Vicky

I'm afraid Pete and Kate get like this sometimes. It's all pretty harmless really

Everyone looks at Vicky

Vicky
I'm Vicky Knight and I have heard all the jokes about shining armour. I am a reporter from the *Sillington Chronicle.* I have worked there for two years after leaving university. I was given this assignment by my editor and so that is why I am here

Peter
To Vicky

Do you have a particular viewpoint on the relationship between social work and the media?

Vicky

No, not really. I haven't come into contact with any social workers. All I know is that when my colleague was working on the Malcolm case that he had great difficulty getting any information from Social Services

Kate

I was the social worker on the case. We were not allowed to talk to the press. I thought it was stupid because what was getting reported was sympathy towards Ted Malcolm. There was a lot more... but we weren't allowed to say and never can.

Confidentiality is such a difficult issue. How can anyone know why we decide things when we are controlled and silenced? I shouldn't even tell you that I was the social worker on the Malcolm case

Peter

I think that we should all agree that whatever is spoken about within this workshop does not go beyond this room

Jane

But how can we trust the reporters amongst us?

Bob

We don't write about everything

Jane

What, only the newsworthy?

Bob

We have to concentrate on current news

Peter

We haven't finished introducing ourselves yet

Kate
Oh Pete does that really matter? What...? Sorry, what's your name?
Looking towards Bob

Bob
Looking at Kate

Bob

Kate
What Bob is saying is crucial to understanding each other... we need to know how we tick

Jane
Yes it's important for us to understand the roots of our work. Bob...

Turning to him

...I'd like to know more

Kate
I'm sure we all would

Everyone looks at Bob

End of scene

Scene five

Back in Vicky and Joshua's bedroom. Joshua is dressed. Vicky is still in bed

Joshua
We'll have to make it up with Lively otherwise we'll get into such a muddle. He's so good at sorting out the other robots when they have problems with their systems. He is the nearest we could get to being human

Vicky
That's why we have been so successful because we got the robots to do the mundane jobs. I know it was political to start with but with the staff shortage…

Joshua
Yes I know. You were saying, about Kate…

Vicky
Yes, she started looking foolish but she talked a lot of sense. Bob was fairly typical of his age group

Joshua
It was ironic that he ended up coming to TV Dementia Care

Vicky
He was sympathetic

Joshua
It didn't appear that way... but we did have some lively discussion anyway

Vicky
You always have to see things with your social work hat on

Joshua
No I don't

Vicky
Oh, come on

Joshua
Let's not argue... we'll have Lively in here sorting us out again

Vicky
Not unless he's turned his audio receptor on again. You know the discussion was going quite well. You were getting on with Bob... both of you were listening to each other.

Joshua
Yes, I suppose there was a good sense of togetherness... and you looked gorgeous in your blue top

Vicky
I thought you were too busy with the discussion

Joshua
We had to size up the enemy

Vicky
Is that what you thought of us?

Joshua
To start with, yes… but, well, you all had a kind of charm, and I suppose it was quite exciting, especially with the TV reporters like Bob

Vicky
You mean we were less glamorous?

Joshua
Playfully

I still fancied you, didn't I?

Vicky
Smiling

Yes, you were very sweet

Joshua
You'll make me throw up in a minute…

Sadly

It all went so well and then disaster struck.... we were so unprepared

End of scene

Scene six

In a large room. People are milling around chatting to each other. There is a row of tables with food and drinks spread along them and people are helping themselves.

Peter is talking to Vicky and Joshua is nearby. Bob is also nearby. Kate goes towards Joshua holding a plateful of food

Kate
Aren't you having something? It's a pretty good spread

Joshua
I'll get something in a minute

Kate
She's very pretty isn't she?

Looking towards Vicky

Joshua
Avoiding Kate's eyes

Yes

Kate
Are you still with Sue?

Joshua
Casually

Yes

Kate
She certainly is very pretty. Perhaps if we had a romance between a social worker and a reporter we could sort all of this out

Joshua
Well what about you with Bob then?

Sarcastically

You like the older man

Kate
I suspect he's married with four kids

Joshua
Nastily

That's never stopped you before

Bob comes towards them with a plateful of food. Kate gives Joshua a dirty look

Kate
Whispering

Don't you dare

Joshua grins back at Kate and goes to talk to a group of people that includes Vicky

Bob
Smiling

It's not as bad as I expected

Kate
To Bob

What isn't?

Bob
Laughing

The food of course... what else do you think I was talking about?

Kate
Sarcastically

When did you say you were retiring?

Bob
I'm semi-retired now... I just do bits

Kate
I suppose you're rich enough to do that... we have to go on to the end... or get burnt out

Bob
Our work has its risks... it's not all plain sailing

Kate
I think I'll get some more food

She moves away from Bob towards the tables laid with the food. Joshua walks towards Bob

Bob
Still no food. Are you on a diet? You look thin enough

Joshua
I thought I would just wait until the queue had disappeared

Bob
That Kate is a lively one...

Joshua
She is, but she's also good at her job... she has brilliant assessment skills. You give her the gist of a case and she'll tell you accurately all the family dynamics

Bob
How old is she?

Joshua
Early thirties I think... she has two youngish teenage kids... why?

Bob
She'd make a good feature and would look good on TV

Joshua
I bet she'd love to do it, but by the time her bosses agreed to it and approved the format you'd be retired

Bob
That's exactly what we've been saying... we give you an opportunity and...

Peter comes towards them

Peter
I thought it went well this morning. I thought that we were getting a good level of understanding between us

Joshua goes to get some food

Bob
I was just saying to…

Looks towards Joshua

…that I think that we could work more with you but….

Peter
Enthusiastically

My colleagues and I in my department would be very interested in working with you. You see, there is a national shortage of social workers and well… perhaps

Bob
Looking towards Kate

Well I was really thinking of someone like Kate. You know, an actual social worker

Peter
Looking miffed

Well… er… well, I think we could be very helpful in an advisory capacity

Enter Ted Malcolm

Bob
Ignoring Peter – looking towards the door

Who's that? He looks very familiar

Ted Malcolm walks past a number of people and heads towards Kate

Peter
I don't know

Changing the subject

I really think that we could work effectively together

Ted
To Kate in a loud voice

It's all right for you being matey with these reporters, but they should know the truth about you

Kate
Looking alarmed

Ted... What are you doing here?

Ted
You are embarrassed by me? You were all friendly before the court case

Kate
Going towards Ted

Look Ted, let's go and have a chat

Ted
No... I've had enough of your little chats

People start noticing the interplay between Ted and Kate

No, that's enough

Ted pulls out a gun and shoots Kate. He drops the gun and doesn't move. Two reporters run towards him, disarm him and push him to the ground.

Ted shouts

She made me do it

People run from everywhere to help Kate. Bob, who's standing near to Joshua, takes his mobile out

Bob
This is Bob. Sally, I need a photographer here at the conference – quickly, a social worker has been shot by a nutter

Joshua
Grabbing the phone off him, shouting

You slime ball, what the hell do you think you are doing?

Bob
It's just my job mate

Joshua
Angrily

But don't you feel anything? Don't you care?

Bob
Look mate, I've been in wars, I've seen far worse than this

Joshua
Angrily

She has two young kids y'know

Bob
It's sad but...

Joshua
It's the story isn't it?

Bob
Of course I sympathise, who wouldn't? But I'm here, I have to do my job

Joshua
That's so cold

Bob
It might seem that way to you but I'm only telling the truth. I'll say she's got two kids and that she was only doing her job

Joshua
But it's only just happening

Bob
That's why it's news... because it's just happening. Those stories you wanted to give us were old

Joshua
But what about people's feelings, the horror, pain, shock, sadness?

Bob
We report so people share those feelings

Joshua
Crying

I don't understand

Vicky comes towards him and puts her arm around him

Vicky
To Bob

He does understand really

End of scene

Scene seven

Back to Joshua and Vicky's bedroom

Joshua
It's strange, the circumstances of life. I don't think that Bob did ever really understand but he did support us later when we started TV Dementia Care. He didn't realise at the time that it was his insurance card.

Vicky
His daughter has been great about letting him be in the ads. We must make sure that when they film again he looks a bit more dignified.

Kate's tragic death had a real impact. In life she was just another social worker but her death happening as it did sent shock waves through the media... people with a conscience began to speak out more... people began to admit to a lack of understanding and co-operation

Joshua
But the thing was that it could have happened to several of us. I was lucky, but some of my colleagues had threats made against them; some had to have protection going in and out of their offices, and yet throughout this they carried on working

Vicky
You make them sound as if they were martyrs

Joshua
Well, I think that some of them were… most people wouldn't put up with what they had to put up with on a regular basis

Vicky
There were other people doing jobs of equal worth; what about the police, doctors and nurses? They did and continue to serve the community

Joshua
But did they get the same level of ridicule or get treated as if they were faceless interfering busy bodies?

Vicky
But many of us were treated the same way… you accused Bob of not caring and yet when you got to know him well you realised that behind that hard exterior there was really a big softy

Joshua
I know, but there were others

Vicky
So you were all perfect?

Joshua
Of course not

Enter Robot Lively

Robot Lively
I was bored and felt it was time that you treated me better

Vicky
I'm sorry Lively, I was worried that you had abandoned us

Robot Lively
Well, I actually came to report that while I've been switched off Robot Billy has tried to act human

Joshua
Oh no, what has he done now?

Robot Lively
I believe that he has muddled up all of the programmes and Bob is currently wondering why he has a date with Doris Day. She will insist on getting him to sing and he really doesn't like it

Joshua
Oh, is that all?

Robot Lively
Oh no, would you like the list?

Vicky
I'm sorry Lively, I promise not to do it again

Robot Lively
You always say that

The end

Collaboration

Core Characters

Joshua
At the beginning he is forty-five years old but is also represented at different younger ages through the series.

He is a sensitive person, rather quiet, a thinker and a bit of a worrier. He has a strong moral base.

He is at times, however, able to talk passionately about things that matter to him, but sometimes he is too selective and jumps to conclusions.

His racial identity could be open to debate.

I had tinkered with the idea of both Joshua and Vicky having dual identity so that it adds to the not fitting in and therefore the attraction to each other.

I haven't thought about his family, as for these episodes it doesn't feel relevant but could easily develop a family around him.

Vicky
As a forty-five-year-old she is a very strong person, she is very bright and able to think quickly and clearly. Although she loves Joshua she can get irritated by his lack of certainty about things. In the episode about disillusionment her doubts could be

expressed through manipulative actions causing her to be a bit of an outcast.

As a twenty-five-year-old she is a conformist but as she gets older she can become more rebellious.

She has a love/hate relationship with Robot Lively.

As with Joshua, I have not given her a family but this can be developed especially perhaps her mother.

Robot Lively
I'm not sure whether it is a he or she, although a friend says it is definitely a he.

Lively always wants to do the right thing and will tell Vicky and Joshua what the right thing is, but he is also loyal to them.

At times he is nearly human but at other times he is clearly a robot. He is the senior robot, keeping all the other ones in order. Some of the episodes, like "Disillusionment", he will only have a minor role, but he is to be there at the beginning of each episode to clearly show the setting of the future.

I hope that he would be a fun part to play and add some humour to balance the seriousness. He is the character for the public to love most.

Episode two of *Collaboration* came easily. It continued the story and seemed to justify that Bob would be part of TV Dementia Care. Whilst I was writing it, I found myself as a middle-aged woman taking on the feelings of Bob the retired man, and had on several occasions to take myself physically away to get out of the character. It was a fascinating and frightening experience.

Episode Two – Bob's Story

By Rachel Bramble

Cast`
Bob – aged eighty-two and sixty-two
Joshua – a man aged forty-five and twenty-five
Robot Lively
Vicky – aged forty-five
Lorraine – Bob's daughter
Bjorn – Lorraine's son
Louise – Bob's wife
Robots
Older people

Scene one

Inside a room with white walls. Images of Doris Day move around the walls.

Bob sits in a comfortable chair gazing at the images. Connected to his fingers is a monitor. There is a small table with a drink on it.

There is a dim but a warm colour lighting the room

End of scene

Scene two

A control room like a studio. There are TV screens showing different rooms with older people in each of them. Robots control the different monitors.

Enter Joshua and Robot Lively

Joshua
Where's Bob then?

Robot Lively
He's in B6 today. Dawn had pre-booked D7, his favourite, and so he wasn't very happy to start with

Joshua
Well he knows that he has to share

Robot Lively
Our home assessment showed that, as a particular individual, he was given a high degree of control over his environment

Joshua
Do you mean that he was spoilt?

Robot Lively
That is not a word in robot vocabulary

Joshua
Looks at the particular screen

He seems all right to me. Perhaps Doris Day is a nice change

Robot Lively
But look at his heart monitor... the reading is rather high

Joshua
That probably means that he just fancies her, that's all

Robot Lively
I don't know what you mean

Joshua
I don't suppose you would. That wouldn't be in your programming system either, would it?

Robot Lively
I believe that you are right there

End of scene

Scene three

Back in the dim lit room known as B6. Bob, who is sitting in the chair, gets up and pulls the monitor from his hand. He knocks over a small table next to him with a drink crashing to the floor

Bob
Shouting

Let me out of here... what are you doing to me?

The door opens and Joshua enters with Robot Lively

Robot Lively
Goes to put monitor back on Bob

Bob... you must stay calm

Bob
Pulls away

Leave me alone, you mechanical know-all

Joshua
Going to Bob touching his arm

It's all right, Bob. Lively was only trying to help you

Bob
Shouting

Help... is that what you call it? Leave me alone.

I want Vicky. Where is Vicky? She understands me best

Joshua
She's gone out for the day with Sally

Bob
Weeping

I want Vicky

Robot Lively
Perhaps I should introduce a cylinder of anti-anxiety chemical

Joshua
Sometimes you really do irritate me Lively. You mean a tranquilliser, don't you?

Robot Lively
You know that in 2016 terminology was removed from the public system

Joshua
Lively, forget it

He turns to Bob

Look Bob, what's wrong?

Bob
It's all of this… it's me… I don't know who I am

Joshua
You are Bob Anderson, an eighty-two-year-old man who lives with his daughter and two grandchildren. You come here just for a change and because you enjoy being cartoon characters.

Unfortunately, today the robots have muddled the different programmes and you were introduced to Doris Day instead of Popeye

Bob
Looking directly at Joshua

But I don't know who I really am. Sometimes I think I do, but the memories are muddled.

I see people… I know names… but it's all muddled

A Tannoy System Announcement:
Well, ladies and gentleman, that is the end of your morning session. We hope that you feel refreshed and ready for your lunch, which will be served in twenty minutes in the dining room

Robot Lively
I will help you Bob

Joshua
No, Lively, leave Bob to me

Robot Lively
But the schedule says that you are with James today

Joshua
Lively, Bob needs me more

Robot Lively
Vicky won't be happy

Joshua
She'll understand… I'll tell her when she comes back.

Please Lively, you charm James for me

Robot Lively
If you mean will I tell him a lie so that he is not distressed then I am not happy about it… but I will

End of scene

Scene four

A dining room with six tables. Each table has older people sitting at it. There are a number of robots serving the tables. In the corner of the room there is a robot playing gentle music on the piano.

Enter Joshua, supporting Bob. He leads him to a table.

Robot Lively enters, supporting another elderly man and helps him to sit at the table

Joshua
Here you are, Bob

Helping him sit down

Bob
Refuses to sit

I don't want to be here. This is not where I live…

Joshua
I know. You are only here for a holiday

Bob
You mean to give my daughter a break?

Joshua
Please Bob, sit down and we will talk after lunch

Bob
It will be too late then. Because I will be like them

Pointing at some of the older people

Joshua
Bob, you need to eat

Bob
Pushing Josh roughly

Leave me alone

Joshua
Pleadingly

Please Bob

Bob pushes Joshua and he falls to the ground. Two robots and Robot Lively rush towards Bob and the two restrain him

Robot Lively
Joshua, you were wrong. I should have handled him

He injects something into Bob's arm. Bob relaxes and is led peacefully to a chair

Joshua
Lively, you shouldn't have done that

Robot Lively
You know the rules in relation to violence

Joshua
But he will never forgive us

Robot Lively
Rules are rules

Joshua
We will never agree about that, will we?

Robot Lively
Looking at Bob

Look Joshua, he is peaceful now. We are supposed to keep people calm

Joshua
I could have calmed him

Robot lively
You can talk to him now he is calm

Joshua
But he won't know me... you know the drug does that

Robot Lively
You can talk to him through his history programme

Joshua
But then I am controlling him and his past

Robot Lively
That was the contract. His daughter comes for him this afternoon. She will not want to cope with his anger

They both look across at him.

The piano player continues playing quiet tunes and the older people eat their food in silence

End of scene

Scene five

An entrance hall outside the dining room. Joshua is standing next to Bob's daughter Lorraine and her son, Bjorn, aged eight years.

Joshua
Hi Lorraine. How are you?

Lorraine
I'm fine thanks

Bjorn starts fiddling with some ornaments on a table in the hall

Bjorn, leave those things alone. They belong to Josie... she won't be very happy if you break them.

I saw Robot Lively and he said that Dad had been rather unsettled

Bjorn fiddles again

Bjorn... I told you to leave them alone... go and talk to Granddad and then you can play in the garden

Bjorn goes into the dining room to see Bob

He said he gave him a jab to calm him down but that you weren't happy about it

Joshua
Well, the law says we have to protect ourselves but... I have known Bob so long and he didn't mean to hurt me

Lorraine
But you said that he has done it before

Joshua
Yes, but it's just frustration... we don't seem to be able to get his programmes right... I often see him in tears... we are supposed to create calm and happiness but sometimes I wonder

Lorraine
But Josh, you know what the alternative was... we wouldn't be allowed to have him at home at all... I want to know my dad in his last few years

Joshua
Could we work together on his programme? You said that you were not in a rush to go home. Lively could get one of the robots to play with Bjorn; they would like that for a change. When it's quiet I often see them trying out children's games

Lorraine
It must get trying for them sometimes, working with all these old people, and they work so many more hours than the humans

Joshua
Watch out Lorraine, you will be getting like me

Lorraine
What do you mean?

Joshua
Treating them the same as humans... Vicky is always reminding me that they are robots and do not have the same rights... but didn't people say the same about black people when our parents were children?

Lorraine
Vicky is very good at what she does and I wouldn't say a word against her as your partner, but I sometimes wonder how you got together. I know you are very happy but her views are often so different to yours... where is she today?

Joshua
Oh she's gone for a girls' day out with Sally. She said that she won't be back till quite late... When Bob had his flip he was asking for her. These old journalists seem to stick together

Bjorn rushes out towards Joshua and Lorraine

Bjorn
Granddad is asking for Louise. Mum, who is Louise?

Lorraine
She is your gran... my mum. She died a long time before you were born, when I was a kid... Go and tell Granddad we will be there in a minute

Bjorn
Okay

He goes back into the dining room. Lorraine and Joshua follow Bjorn

End of scene

Scene six

In the dining room. Bob, robots, Robot Lively, Lorraine, Joshua, Bjorn, older people. Same set. Lorraine goes towards Bob

Lorraine
Hi Dad

Gives him a kiss

How are you?

Bob looks into thin air and doesn't respond

End of scene

Scene seven

In a dining room, same set as Episode One. Bob, Joshua, Vicky and people from the conference. Lots of people buzzing around. Kate is lying on the floor surrounded by people.

Bob
Aged Sixty-two on his mobile

Where is the photographer I asked for?

Joshua
How could you? How could you?

End of scene

Scene eight

Back in the dining room. Same set and people as Scene six

Lorraine
Dad, it's me, Lorraine

Bob looks into thin air

Dad, it's me… don't you know me?

Bob looks straight through Lorraine

Joshua
Lively, quick – get Bob to a TV room

Lively
But they are all pre-booked

Joshua
Just find one… that's an order

Bob looks into thin air

Lorraine
Getting tearful

Dad… Oh Josh, I didn't want it to be this way… we promised him that he would be with Mum

Joshua
Shouting

Lively, this is an emergency… get that room now!

Robot Lively
Okay

Bob continues to look into thin air. Two robots come and put him into a wheelchair

Joshua
To Lively, whispering

How much did you give him?

Robot Lively
The blue dosage

Joshua
Oh no, you fool! He had been changed to yellow… he has had a build-up… We will have to get his super-stimulation programme going

Lorraine
Is he going to be all right?

Joshua
We are going for the super programme

Lorraine
But you know what happens if he requests that one

Joshua
I know... Vicky will go mad at me, but it's the only way to get him back

Joshua
Lively, it's the super programme

They push Bob out of the room

End of scene

Scene nine

Bob is in the TV room sitting in a comfy chair with lights flashing around the room. He is wired to a receptor.

He gets up and walks around the room. Returns to the chair

Bob
Louise darling, don't do that now. Come and sit with me

End of scene

Scene ten

In the control room. Robot Lively, Joshua, Bob and Louise, and another robot. They are watching Bob as a vision of Louise appears in front of Bob and on all of the walls

Joshua
It's working

Lorraine
Thank God... I thought I had lost him this time

Robot Lively
Joshua... this is the fifth time... the contract says only six and then no more

Joshua
Damn the contract... If we can bring him back I'll do it twenty times

Lorraine
But Josh, I don't want you to get into trouble

Joshua
Bob's a friend. Besides, it's time the law was changed anyhow. Look at Bob – he is happy. As long as we get a good report back from him, we will be okay

We'll do it together shall we Louise?

Louise
Yes, I'd like that

Joshua
Lively, we'll leave him for another twenty minutes

Robot Lively
You are pushing it a bit aren't you?

Joshua
Don't worry… it will be okay

To Lorraine

Let's go and have a drink. We'll see you later Lively

Exit Joshua and Lorraine. Lively continues to monitor Bob

End of scene

Scene eleven

In the hallway. There are some older people and robots wandering around. Enter Vicky in a rushed state

Vicky
To a Robot

Where's Lively or Josh?

Robot
Lively is in C10 with Bob

Vicky runs up the hall, throwing the coat at a stand

End of scene

Scene twelve

The monitor room. Lively and two other Robots. Enter Vicky

Vicky
Lively, what happened?

Robot lively
I gave him some blue and he was supposed to have yellow

Vicky
Never mind about that now… what has Bob said?

Robot Lively
We haven't talked to him yet… Joshua and Louise were going to do that

Vicky
Okay, where are they?

Robot Lively
Having a drink

Vicky goes to a microphone

Vicky
Through the microphone

Josh… contact me in C10 now.

Lively, how long as he had?

Robot Lively
Thirty-seven minutes

Vicky
You'd better stop then. I'll go in and see him

End of scene

Scene thirteen

In the TV room C10. Bob sits looking into thin air. Vicky goes and sits next to Bob

Vicky
Bob… You okay?

Bob sits looking into thin air

How was Louise today? Was she busy or did you have a chance just to sit and chat?

Bob continues to look into thin air. The door bursts open and enter Joshua and Lorraine

Louise
Hi, Vicky. Did you have a good day out?

Vicky
It was fine. I've been talking to Bob but he hasn't responded

Bob continues to look into thin air

Joshua
Lively gave him the wrong dose

Vicky
I know, he told me… You took a risk giving him so long an awareness dose

Joshua
But Vicky, it's Bob… I had to do the best I could for him. Have you forgotten our twenty-year history?

Vicky
Of course not. That's why I came back early because I thought Bob might not talk to you. I didn't know that Lorraine was here

Joshua
Look at Bob

Bob looks towards Vicky and Joshua and smiles

End of scene

Scene fourteen

Bob sits looking at a hologram of Louise and smiles

Joshua
Vicky... Bob is happy

Vicky
How do you know?

Joshua
Just look at his eyes

Enter Lorraine and Bjorn

I'm sorry Lorraine, he's gone. He's with your mum now

Lorraine
But he's happy, Josh... it's where he wants to be

Bob continues to smile at Louise. The others leave and Bob smiles

The end

Chapter 5
Letter to MPs

After some discussion Stephen and I decided to write to all Members of Parliament to try to encourage them to help build a better relationship between their local Social Services and their local media. Our letter is reproduced below. Of the six hundred and fifty-nine MPs, we had a hundred and fifty-nine replies, of which about fifty-five were very encouraging. At the time of writing this we have had no more replies.

The House of Commons
Westminster
London

20 February 2002

Dear

A Fresh Start and a Positive Approach

As a qualified Social Worker and Practice Teacher with over a quarter of a century of experience working both for Social Services and in voluntary organisations I am writing to promote positive working between Social Work and the Media.

With an ageing population and an increasing number of alienated young people the pressures on both Social Workers and resources are reaching their limit.

Although Social Services Departments provide services nationally to the most vulnerable members of the community the amount of press and air time that is given is minimal. This has led to ignorance and poor stereotyping of the role of social workers and stigmatising of service users.

You are a person in a position of power and are able to effect change through:

1. encouraging television, radio and newspapers in your constituency to carry regular stories about work carried out by their local Social Services, and

2. request the inclusion of how to work with the media as a component of the new three year social work course to enable qualified Social Workers to have a greater understanding of the role of the media and how to build positive links.

Most Social Workers are both fearful of and ignorant of the role of the media and this is their downfall because if they were able to face members of the media on a regular basis the truth about our worth would come out and the people we work with would become far less stigmatised and could lead happier lives.

I draw your attention to a new website dedicated to positive working relations between social work and the media to be launched shortly, www.scampweb.com

Thank you.

Chapter 6
SCAMP

I don't know whether it was Stephen or me that thought about having a website to get across some of my ideas about social work and the media.

It sounded a brilliant idea and I began to write stuff. We bought the site www.scampweb.org. It took us ages to get the name, as I wanted to combine letters that related to social work and the media. We tried things like "SWIM" but found that they all sounded a little negative, but then I thought of "SCAMP", meaning "Social Care and Media People". It seemed just right, and it also gave the imagery of someone who was a little naughty but also nice.

Unfortunately, Stephen and I splitting up has led to the delay (or demise) of SCAMP. I hope that SCAMP will come to fruition some day, but I'm afraid that I am the ideas person and am hopeless with a computer, so if Stephen doesn't do it I'll need some help.

Below are some of the original ideas for SCAMP.

The aim of SCAMP

The aim of SCAMP is to provide a website where the image of social work and social care, and in particular that of social workers, can be explored.

The site also aims to be proactive and look positively at how to increase public knowledge of the work that social workers undertake and to enable a higher profile in all forms of media. The site will have a number of aspects to include:

- political aspects of the work;
- social work on TV, radio and in the newspapers;
- statistical information about social care workers;
- links to other sites;
- innovations; and
- intellectual debates.

Just a normal day

With Tweedledee and Tweedledum, and Mrs Jones. Not two fat boys but two challenging boys.What do you do with two twelve-year-old boys who no one wants to look after?

They wreak havoc wherever they go. They go into foster care and terrorise, they go back home and destroy car windows and trash the living room. Two boys totally out of control, but it is the social worker who ultimately has to decide their fate. But there is a shortage of social workers and so one worker sits for over two hours deciding with the manager how to fit the fate of Tweedledee and Tweedledum into the week's schedule and the other eighty-four children who need his help.

He is told to get them a placement come what may, and so he attends the funding panel, who reluctantly give him the £3500 a week for each child. They know full well that this is starving the budgets and so they ask him to return in a month's time with a more cost-effective solution.

Meanwhile, down the road his partner is attending her panel. Mrs Jones is no longer able to manage at home and would like to go to The Croft. It costs £350 per week, which is above the allowance that the local authority will pay. Mrs Jones worked all of her life but only has her State pension. Her family has been told that they will have to contribute towards her fees and they have worked out how they can scrape together the extra £40 a week between them, especially difficult since Joe was made redundant.

That night it's a chippy for tea. Both workers are knackered. Both got their money but it took so much of their time that the former only saw two of the other eighty-four and the latter was half an hour late to see Mr Smith, whose daughter wasn't at all happy. But then they say it's just a normal day.

SCAMP

Challenging the perceptions of social care and social work through building positive links with the media.

Who is it for?

SCAMP is being devised to be of interest to anyone who works in either social care or the media. It should also be of interest to the general public, Members of Parliament and academics, both in social work and courses dedicated to the training of reporters and other forms of media.

What is it about?

SCAMP will describe the everyday situations, frustrations and human nature of social work and social care, and examine different aspects and images of social care and social work in the press and on TV and radio. It will encourage an exchange of information between the many functions within the social care fields and the formats required by different parts of the media. To create a better understanding of the needs of the media and those of social care. It will encourage innovation in drama, documentaries and news, to enable the public to have a better understanding of the complex nature and issues in social care.

Why?

There is extremely little coverage of social care news in the mass media and often what is reported is the crisis rather than the everyday. There has never been a TV drama series which puts social workers as the core characters. Documentaries are few and far between and are often as a result of tragedies or are transmitted at non-peak viewing times. There is a national shortage of social workers and so there is a risk of standards dropping. There is also a high incidence of illness amongst social workers and an increase in pressure of work both in the areas of children/family work and work with adults. Social care has as many interesting stories as any other group in society but social workers generally fear the media due to a lack of mutual understanding of each other's roles in society.

Where/how?

SCAMP will gather stories, ideas and information from a variety of sources, but also hopes to be interactive. The webmaster will try to answer requests for information or put workers from the media in touch with workers from social care.

Postscript note

After Stephen and I split up I attempted to keep him interested in the website, but it was hopeless and nearly a year on I had to admit to failure. Perhaps one day I will find someone who can help me again. If anyone is interested, has the time and/or resources, email me: rachelbramble@yahoo.co.uk

Never-ending

Social work is not a project, it is an existence, in the sense that people will always need someone to help them. There will always be people who at some time in their life need guidance and support from a stranger, and who better than a social worker; someone who looks at that person as an individual with their own specific needs, not someone who is ill, just someone who cannot cope with either what is expected of them or the norms of the community that they belong to. Belonging in itself is so important and as the nameless social worker I have often wondered where I belonged and so can understand what it is like to be a misfit, but I suppose that what we all seek in life is complete fulfilment and happiness, whether that is material or spiritual or both. So I finish this book with the hope that social work will remember its human roots and have the guts and courage to challenge anyone or anything that lets the Robot Livelys take over. I have had lots of happiness and sadness in my life and I expect this to continue. I cannot fully protect my children from the world and I am no saint when it comes to being a mother, but I can at least try to bring open discussion and hope to people's lives.

The future

I am committing seven more years to social work and then I am going to live by the sea and become bewitched by the waves. I want to leave social work as an accepted and respected profession where social workers become recognised as being as important as GPs and all sorts of social workers appear in both reality TV and TV dramas and series.

The document "Every Child Matters" and the "Children's Bill" which is expected to be the new Children Act 2004 has a great deal that I believe in, in terms of multidisciplinary working but to make it work systems just have to be simplified.

I recently wrote to the Prime Minister about the need to simplify and got a reply from the Communications Unit at 10 Downing St. acknowledging my letter and saying it was the responsibility of the Department of Health. The next day I got another letter from a different worker in the same unit saying it was the responsibility of the Department of Education and Skills. A week later I got a letter from the Department of Education and Skills saying that it was the responsibility of the Department of Health. We are all human, but what does this say about Social Work? Does the interest of government only reflect that of the media. In other words MPs, like the media, expect the impossible and that the faceless social workers protect the vulnerable but when things go wrong they become the scapegoats for a system which is basically a form of organised chaos. I hope not.

Rachel Bramble